Adventures in

MATHOPOLIS

PARTING IS SUCH SWEET SORROW

FRACTIONS AND DECIMALS

Linda Powley
and Catherine Weiskopf
Illustrated by Tom Kerr

BARRON'S

All inquiries should be addressed to:
Barron's Educational Series, Inc.
250 Wireless Boulevard
Hauppauge, New York 11788
www.barronseduc.com

ISBN-13: 978-0-7641-4171-3
ISBN-10: 0-7641-4171-6

Library of Congress Catalog Card No.: 2008019856

Library of Congress Cataloging-in-Publication Data
Powley, Linda.
    Adventures in mathopolis : parting is such sweet sorrow : fractions and decimals / Linda Powley and Catherine Weiskopf.
        p. cm.
    ISBN-13: 978-0-7641-4171-3
    ISBN-10: 0-7641-4171-6
    1.   Fractions—Juvenile   literature.   2.   Decimal fractions—Juvenile   literature.   I. Weiskopf, Catherine.
    II. Title
QA117.P69   2009
513.2'6—dc22   2008019856

Printed in the United States of America
9 8 7 6 5 4 3 2 1

Table of Contents

Chapter 1: Career Week   1

Chapter 2: A Place for Everything; Everything in Its Place   7

Chapter 3: Make a Long Story Half as Short   18

Chapter 4: Hi Ho, High Low, It's Off to Think We Go   29

Chapter 5: Mixin' Things Up   41

Chapter 6: Searching for Equals   57

Chapter 7: It's Not Easy Being Common   74

Chapter 8: Out of Order   84

Chapter 9: It All Adds Up   99

Chapter 10: Turbo Fractions   116

Chapter 11: The Flip Side   124

Chapter 12: Parting Is Such Sweet Sorrow   134

Chapter 12.5: Right on the Money   146

Chapter 13: Line 'Em Up   156

Chapter 14: As Easy as Pie   169

Chapter 15: Turbo Dot Speed   179

Chapter 16: Converts   193

Chapter 17: All's Well That Ends Well   210

Chapter 1
Career Week

"Holy Moley, class! Settle down," Mr. Little said, clapping his hands together three times. At four feet, ten inches, he definitely lived up to his name, but he was a good, experienced teacher.

"As you know," he began after the students got mostly still, "today is the beginning of Career Week, and we have with us the mayor of Mathopolis, Lostis Marbles. Let's give him a warm welcome."

The class clapped politely.

"Thank you," Mr. Little said. "Now, Mayor, can you tell us how you use math in your position as city leader?" He got down off his stool and sat behind his desk while Mayor Marbles fumbled with some papers.

"Not a speech," complained a boy name Sticky sitting in the back. It wasn't his real name, of course, but everyone called him that because trouble seemed to stick to him like glue. "Learning about careers is supposed to be fun."

Mayor Marbles stuffed his papers into his pocket and decided to ad-lib. "We use math a lot at City Hall. After all, this is Mathopolis! We use math when we uhm, —"

"Excuse me, Mr. Mayor, but don't you use it to make decisions and pay the city's bills?" said a very proper girl sitting near the front. Her name was Egweena.

Trusty Dusty, the mayor's faithful assistant, touched his boss on the arm. "If you don't mind, sir."

Relieved, Mayor Marbles stepped back.

"Okay," Trusty said. "Math is used in a lot of ways in the mayor's office. Say the city wants to build a soccer field, and we can't decide whether it should go on Elm Street or Oak Street." He began pacing back and forth, like teachers do sometimes.

"Well, we'd take a poll and ask our citizens for their wishes. Say half of the citizens wanted the field built on Elm Street, a third wanted it built on Oak Street, and the rest didn't care. We'd know to build on Elm Street."

"Why?" asked the hungry voice.

"Because everyone on Oak Street is a loser," Sticky called from the back, and the students erupted.

He had it!

"I need twelve volunteers," he announced.

"Me, me, me," voices shouted as chairs scraped and students bumped to the front.

"Okay," Trusty said, once the students had gathered. "How many students do you see?"

"Twelve," several voices shouted.

"Now let's make two groups of six." The students scrambled around until they'd made the change. "See?" Trusty went on. "We now have two groups, each with half of our volunteers."

Everyone nodded.

"Now say we want a third of our volunteers in one group, and half in another. How would we do that?" The twelve students began to mill around. Three broke off from one group and one from another.

"No, no," Trusty said, "We need four from one group, and six to stay in the other. The last two will be all by themselves."

"Mr. Dusty?" Ms. Shabang, the teacher's aide, quietly interrupted. "Why don't I take the class on to PE?"

"Good idea," Trusty said, and without even waiting to line up the students bolted out the door.

"Ms. Shabang is a great helper," Mr. Little assured Mayor Marbles when he got back from the principal's office. "She'll get the students to channel their energy correctly."

He nodded toward the window. Outside all the students except two had linked together in a big circle. The two not in the circle were holding hands while they roamed around the outer side.

"I remember this game," Trusty said. "We used to call it the Flying Dutchman. It was a lot of fun."

"It looks like she's trying to get them to do something else," the mayor observed.

And indeed, she was.

"Children, let's all gather in a line and do jumping jacks," Shabang insisted, "We haven't warmed up."

"Naw," one called.

"We want to do this," another said.

Before Ms. Shabang could say another thing, Egweena, who was one of the students in the pair circling the group, raised her hand and chopped through the link formed by two of her friends.

"You're it!" Egweena said, and she and her partner took off running. The two whose chain she'd broken fumbled around, rejoined hands, and flew off the other way.

The race was on.

But something was wrong.

Just as quickly as she had changed, Ms. Shabang recovered. She pulled herself upright, smoothed her one-piece dress, and walked back to the circle. Egweena and her partner made it back first and joined hands with their companions to complete the link. Now the two who had lost the race were roaming the outside, and again Ms. Shabang was petitioning them to stop and do warm-ups.

The dog, Mongrel, watched from his spot on the sidewalk. This wasn't the first time he'd seen Shabang act this way. Something definitely wasn't right.

He turned and trotted off into the park, stopping at a small, hidden clearing by the pond. No one was in sight, and it was time to get help. He lifted his muzzle to the sky and let out one long, mournful howl.

Chapter 2

A Place for Everything;
Everything in Its Place

"Perfect," Ms. Shabang thought as she ran her hands down the sides of the dress. Not a wrinkle in sight. Her hair, pulled back in a tight bun, was perfect, too. Not a strand out of place.

All her life she'd had to share her food, her clothes, her toys. Growing up with nine sisters and four brothers meant nothing was completely hers.

When her mother bought a package of ten hair bows, Shabang only got $\frac{1}{10}$. The other $\frac{9}{10}$ went to her sisters. If she was assigned the task of splitting a bag of peanuts fairly between herself and her brothers, she did all the work but only got $\frac{1}{5}$ of the treats!

No more.

She was on her own now, and she could have the whole, the entire uncut sandwich. She could enjoy the complete, undamaged piece of fruit. No longer did she have to split anything with anyone.

Her face twitched at the word *split,* and she shook a little. Strange. Yesterday she had that weird attack when the children were playing the Flying Dutchman, and today this.

Something seemed to be going on, something she couldn't quite put her finger on, but she'd think about it later. It was time to get moving, or she'd be late for school. There was always so much to do at the beginning of the day. She had to make sure everything was in its place.

One tiny hair fell down across her forehead.

"Can't have that," she said. Carefully she smoothed it back against her head, opened the top bureau drawer, and frowned.

She picked up a hairpin that had fallen in with her rubber bands and put it where it belonged. "Matching units must stay together," she said as if the hairpin was in trouble for being with the rubber bands.

Then she counted her four cans of hairspray that were lined up side by side. "One can, two cans, three cans, and four," she said, pulling out the last can of spray. She took off the cap, and held her breath.

Whew! It's a good thing she got out of there while she could still breathe!

Besides, what was she talking about? Units? Counting her cans of hairspray? You may think that Shabang wasn't saying anything important about math, but truth is she has a couple of good points. So let's review these points, and a few others, before you enter into the world of fractions and decimals. If you know anything at all about whole numbers you can bring that knowledge with you.

Let's take out the first sign from the Knowledge of Whole Numbers cart.

Every digit makes different numbers depending on the place it occupies.

And when you add fractions and decimals to the possible places a digit can occupy, it can mean even smaller amounts.

Let's have a look at how this works with decimals.

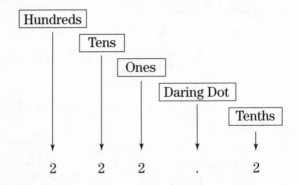

Since twos seem to have taken over this page, we need to talk about what the illustration above means. Depending on the place the two occupies, it could mean two hundreds, two tens, two ones, or two tenths. But since we are talking about pages, all together the number means 222.2 pages.

When you work with the digit two—

Okay. When you work with three and five, what whole numbers can you make?

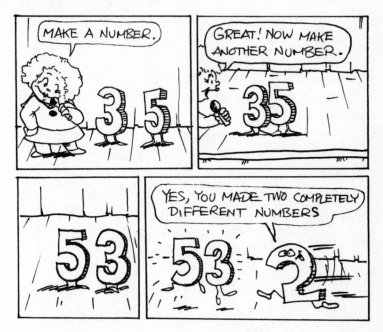

When we work with fractions and decimals, any digits (like the digits three and five) can be in a fraction or decimal. Where they are placed will make all the difference in the world of pancakes.

See how easy it was to review place?

Next up are *units*. Even if you've never heard of units, you have worked with them.

The definition of a unit is anything you call *one*. When you measure, you decide on the unit of measurement. What do you call one? An inch? A foot? A mile?

What is the measurement of a piece of licorice? If you say five, it means nothing without its unit. Five inches is a lot different than five feet or five miles.

When you need to talk about how much pizza you have, your unit can be one slice of the pizza, the whole pizza, or all the pizzas that were ordered for the party.

Whatever unit you pick determines how you count your pizza. Say you want to determine how much Mayor Marbles ate. If your unit is a slice of whole bean anchovy dill pickle pizza (BAD pizza), you will count them like this: "1 slice, 2 slices, 3 slices, 4 slices, 5 slices, 6 slices, 7 slices, and 8 slices."

If your unit is a pizza divided into eight pieces, you will count $\frac{1}{8}$, $\frac{2}{8}$, etc.

If your unit is the whole group of ten BAD pizzas that were ordered for the party, you will count it differently.

It may not seem very important, this thing called units, but it is. And it will be especially important later on when you work with fractions. When you worked with units in the past, you were aware that they had to be the same.

Say you were comparing your weight with the weight of your sister. You want to find out how much heavier she is than you are.

You weighed yourself and found you were sixty-eight pounds. Your sister insisted on being weighed in kilograms because they are more flattering. She weighs forty-five kilograms. Now you need to find the difference in your weight.

If you didn't think the unit was important you'd subtract 68 pounds – 45 kilograms = 23.

You know it doesn't make sense to add or subtract pounds and kilograms, because they aren't in the same unit of measurement, so the answer has no meaning. You'd need to convert her weight to pounds or yours to kilograms for it to make sense.

IN CASE YOU CAN'T LEAVE THIS PROBLEM UNTIL YOU KNOW WHO IS HEAVIER.

45 KILOGRAMS = ABOUT 99 POUNDS SO 99 - 68 = 31 POUNDS. HIS SISTER IS 31 POUNDS HEAVIER THAN HE IS.

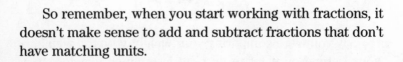

So remember, when you start working with fractions, it doesn't make sense to add and subtract fractions that don't have matching units.

Take, for example, the fraction problem of $\frac{1}{2} + \frac{3}{5}$. You just can't add the top numbers and get four. You have to make each fraction have the same units.

> JUST IN CASE YOU CAN'T MOVE ON WITHOUT
> KNOWING THE ANSWER: $\frac{1}{2} + \frac{3}{5} = \frac{5}{10} + \frac{6}{10} = \frac{11}{10}$

Finally, let's review something you've been doing since you were three. Let's review counting.

Of course you can count, but you need to notice what happens when you count. Say you are counting by one, and you begin to count your butterscotch squares 1, 2, 3, 4, 5, 6, 7, 8, 9. What happens after the nine?

Because the whole numbers are based on ten, every time they complete a group of ten, you have a whole group of ten, and you start over with a new group of ten: 11, 12, 13, 14, 15, 16, 17, 18, 19. That nine tells us that with one more piece of butterscotch candy, we will have another group of ten, and the next number will bump the tens place up to a two.

How does this apply to fractions? Well, if your unit has been divided by ten, and you want to count by $\frac{1}{10}$, you start with $\frac{1}{10}, \frac{2}{10}, \frac{3}{10}, \frac{4}{10}$, and you keep going until you get to $\frac{10}{10}$. When you get to $\frac{10}{10}$, the tenths are too big to be counted individually and need to be counted as a whole one. This happens with fractions when the top number is the same as the bottom number.

If you are counting with the fraction $\frac{1}{3}$, you would count $\frac{1}{3}, \frac{2}{3}, 1, 1\frac{1}{3}, 1\frac{2}{3}, 2$. Every time the numerator and denominator denominator are the same you have a whole group, and you bump up the whole number.

How would you count $\frac{1}{7}$ all the way until you get to 2?

Are you ready to enter the world of fractions and decimals?

Did you keep your units together, like Shabang? Do you have a place for everything, and everything in its place?

Then let's follow Silver and have some fun!

Chapter 3
Make a Long Story Half as Short

"Oh, will you look at this?" Mayor Marbles said, taking a good whiff of a pecan pie he'd pulled out of the basket. For a superhero, Dixie sure could cook, and he was glad she'd agreed to help him with the annual Mathopolis barbecue.

And Dixie Dot liked to cook, too: chicken fried steak, black-eyed peas, catfish, fried okra, butter beans, sweet tea, rhubarb pie, anything and everything from a Southern kitchen.

"That pie looks so perfect I hate for you to cut it," Mayor Marbles said.

"No cutting needed." Dixie smiled and took her special pen, Dot Power, out from behind her ear. She adjusted its setting to one-tenth, aimed and fired right at the pie. It wasn't a bullet that came out of the pen, or a spit wad, or a period; it was a decimal, and when it hit the pie, the pie split into ten equal pieces.

"Ready to serve," the mayor said, setting the pie aside so he could look deeper into the basket.

"What time does the barbecue start?" Dixie asked as the mayor straightened up. She hoisted the basket onto her right shoulder.

"About the same time you finish the cornbread," the mayor said hopefully.

"You mean this cornbread?" Dixie pulled a card out of her pocket.

The mayor took a look and scratched his head. "I've never seen a recipe like this."

"Guess you'd have to know my Mama," Dixie said, laughing. "Sometimes she uses decimals like 0.5 cups of flour, and sometimes she uses fractions like $\frac{1}{2}$ tsp of sugar."

"Right. I see it now," the mayor said. "We'd better hurry on to City Hall's kitchen and get started."

Dixie was only half a step behind, easily carrying the heavy food basket, when she froze.

Quickly she set the basket down and raced over to where Silver stood.

"The school yard!" she said, yanking at his arm. "Someone's in trouble!"

"Go," Silver shouted. He never was one to mince words.

"Add more sugar to the batter," Dixie called to the mayor as she turned toward the school. Since it was only a few blocks away, it was faster to just run.

So while the mayor whips up the cornbread on his own, and the heroes rush to the rescue, let's use the time to delve a bit further into the world of fractions and decimals.

To think fractions and decimals are cool, you have to actually like parts, like a part of the whole or a part of the set, like part of the whole enchilada, part of the whole buttermilk biscuit, or part of a whole cup of lemonade.

You may remember your teacher saying that a set is a group of objects or people that have something in common, and that is correct. Together sets are considered the whole thing: a set of fifth graders or a set of silverware.

Part of the set of the fifth grade class is girls, and part of the set of silverware is forks.

Having part of a thing is different from having (or talking about) the whole thing, or whole set. In fact, the word for fraction comes from the Latin word *fractio*, which means to *break*, and that's what fractions do. They break a whole into parts.

The word decimal comes from the Latin word *decima*, which means *tenth*, and that's what decimals do. They break something into tenths or hundredths, thousandths, and it just keeps on going. (You keep going by dividing the last number by ten.)

With fractions you can divide the whole into the number of pieces you want. With decimals the pieces are divided into multiples of ten.

DECIMALS ARE REALLY JUST DECIMAL FRACTIONS. THEY ARE FRACTIONS THAT HAVE A DENOMINATOR THAT IS A POWER OF TEN.

Fractions and decimals are two different languages, but both talk about having part of something. And it's important to learn how to talk the language of fractions and decimals because they are everywhere! Money uses decimals: $1.23 is equal to one whole dollar and $\frac{23}{100}$ of the next dollar. You need to use decimals to figure out how much each of five girls needs to chip in to buy Dixie a new cookbook that costs $12.35.

$12.35 \div 5 = \$2.47$

And you can't forget that Dixie uses fractions and decimals to cook. Well, she does some of the time.

You use fractions and decimals when you talk to your parents about your fair share of the ice-cream cake. You also use them to measure out ingredients for your volcano science project, divide numbers that don't come out even like 6 ÷ 4 = 1.5, and measure out boards to build a tree house. Decimals are also part of taking your temperature with a thermometer.

Before we move on, let's have a glance at how fractions and decimals look because while they tell us the same thing, they look very different.

Fractions are tall and look like a bunk bed. Decimals are short and wide like a beanbag chair with numbers leaking out the end of it. Here come Dixie and Silver to demonstrate.

This whole book will explain more about how to write, to say, and to make fractions and decimals. But first, look at the number line below to see that even though they look very different, they both are talking about the same thing.

$$\frac{1}{4} \qquad \frac{1}{2} \qquad \frac{3}{4}$$

0   0.25   0.5   0.75

PAUSE FOR THOUGHT

You can see by the number line that $\frac{1}{4}$ is the same as saying 0.25. So could $0.75 or 75 cents be written as a part of a dollar? (*Hint:* Use the number line.)

$\frac{3}{4}$ of a dollar

Notice, that before fractions and decimals came along there was a lot of empty space on the number line between the whole numbers.

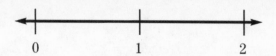

With fractions and decimals, all that space between the whole numbers can be filled. The whole numbers themselves can even have different fraction or decimal names.

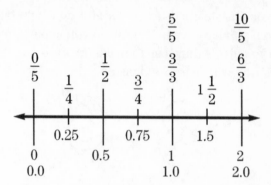

The fraction $\frac{6}{3}$ is also the whole number two. The decimal 2.0 is also the whole number two. Fractions and decimals are not only in between zero and one, they can be zero and one, when zero is written, for example, as $\frac{0}{2}$ or 0.0 and one is expressed as $\frac{2}{2}$ or 1.0.

Note that with decimals the part after the Daring Dot, or decimal point, can never be greater than one. It can get very close, but it can never quite get there.

0.99999999 ≈ 1

As you just learned, fractions and decimals talk about parts. So if you have a whole, how do you make it into parts? How do you divide things up to make fractions and decimals?

Well, one way is to use division.

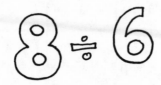

8 ÷ 6

You could fold, or draw a line, or do many other things, but no matter how you divide things, it still doesn't change the whole. Say you have three sandwiches: one you divide into two parts, one you divide into four parts, and one you divide into one hundred parts.

2 PARTS   4 PARTS   100 PARTS

26

If you ate two parts of the first sandwich, your friend ate four parts of the second, and Mongrel ate one hundred parts of the third, who ate more of the sandwich? You ate two halves, your friend ate four fourths, and Mongrel ate a hundred hundredths. You all ate the same amount because you all ate the whole thing. The number of pieces the sandwich was divided into was the only thing different.

Now you try one. Say you have a pizza. Which is more, $\dfrac{7}{7}$ or $\dfrac{8}{8}$ of the pizza?

They are both the same.

No matter how you divide it, the whole thing is still the whole thing.

Finally, here's a warning about this book. It is not about whole things. It's about parts—parts of watermelons, parts of dog bones, parts of hot dogs, and even parts of quickly growing plants. In fact, even this book was written in parts by a team of two people, just like Dixie Dot and Silver Splitter are a team of superheroes, handling a crisis. Well, maybe it's not a crisis.

"Guess what," Dixie said, taking the proper time to swallow her food before speaking. "It was all a false alarm. Sticky called us to the school to see how fast we could get there."

Trusty shook his head. "What if someone had needed you? And you'd been off on a wild goose chase."

"Exactly," Silver said, reaching for the whole plate of homemade cookies.

"I hope Mr. Little took care of him," the mayor said.

"Oh, yes. Sticky had to go to the principal's office, and they called his parents. But you know what?" Dixie asked.

"What's that?" Trusty answered, watching Silver scarf down his treats.

"Just once, I wish we had a real crisis, not where anyone got hurt or anything, but one that would really test our skills." Dixie said.

"Your hearing," Silver said.

"Your speed," Dixie agreed.

"And your strength," Silver sighed, and they both fell quiet with their own thoughts.

But hmm, what is that old saying? The one your grandmother likes to say? Something about being careful what you wish for?

Aww—, yes, that's it.

And maybe Dixie should have listened to *her* grandmother because it won't be long before she and Silver find that what they wished for has come true.

Hi Ho, High Low, It's
Off to Think We Go

"Not Sticky?" Silver asked as he navigated his way down the street.

"No," Dixie said, glancing out the side window. "It's real. And this is the day Mr. Little is taking his class to the bank on a field trip."

Silver mashed the accelerator to the floor while Dixie leaned back against the headrest and pressed her legs into the floorboard.

When they'd gone $\frac{7}{10}$ of the way, that's seven out of ten blocks, Silver asked, "Hear?"

Dixie held up her index finger and leaned in toward the window. "Oh, Silver. A proper sounding voice is telling someone to open the vault."

"How many?"

Dixie listened hard. "Three, maybe four. We need to hurry."

A bank robbery!

Wow!

Dixie and Silver definitely have the mission for which they'd wished! But while we wait for them to get to the bank, let's learn more about fractions.

In the last chapter, we saw that a fraction looks a lot like a bunk bed because it was two stories and all. Instead of one bed on top of another, though, a fraction has one number on top of another. Instead of being called bottom and top bunk, each place has a special name.

Like the kids yelling out of their beds say, the upper level is called the numerator, and the bottom level is called the denominator. If you have trouble remembering which part of the fraction is the denominator, remember *down* and *denominator* start with the same letter.

Both the numerator and denominator have a job only they can do. Let's take a closer look.

First, let's start with the denominator. One way to think of it is to use the word *total*. The total number of equal pieces, or parts, that something has been divided into is the denominator.

And almost anything can be divided into parts: a grilled cheese sandwich, a whole apple, or a whole set of marbles. And the key word to this division is equal. If they aren't equal parts, then you aren't talking fractions.

Although it's often hard to be exact, you must at least give it a try. You can't call any part a half just because you're sharing it between two people.

Say you want to divide something to share. The more people you want to share with, the more equal pieces, or parts, you will need. More pieces mean a bigger denominator. You may have grown up thinking that bigger is always more and better, but this isn't always true.

In fact, the opposite is true: Bigger is smaller when it comes to denominators. Remember Shabang, who grew up with all those brothers and sisters?

Sadly for Shabang, they didn't stop at eight children, so when they had nine, how much did each child get? And when they had ten?

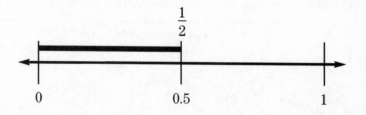

Perhaps you need a number line to help you see how a bigger denominator means a smaller cut. When the only child got the whole cake, it looks like this on the number line. She got all of it from zero to one.

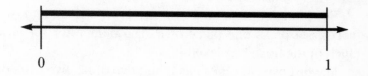

0　　　　　　　　　　　　　　　1

When a second child was born, she had to split the whole, and her share of the whole cake would be:

$$\frac{1}{2}$$

0　　　　　　　0.5　　　　　　1

And, after her eighth sister was born, her share would go down to a wee little bit.

33

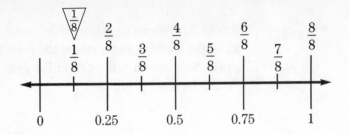

Before going on, let's look at one more quick point about the denominator. The only number that can't be a denominator is zero. Think about it. You can't divide a waffle into zero pieces because zero means you have nothing to divide.

Moving on, right above the denominator, on the upper level, is the numerator. Numerators tell you how many parts of the whole or parts of the set someone has. Think of the numerator as a picky person who is selective in how many items she wants.

Say Mongrel has a bone that has been divided into two pieces. He picks one piece of it. The numerator for how much of the bone he picked is one.

Mayor Lostis Marbles has found two of his five pairs of glasses. Therefore, the numerator for how many glasses he has found is two.

Whatever you have divided, the numerator tells you how many parts of the whole are being referenced.

Remember how the piece of the pie got smaller when the denominator got bigger? With numerators, bigger is better—unless you're talking about something you want to share like work or peas.

For good things, though, a bigger numerator means more of the enchilada, more of the pie, more of the hot tamales. But you never get back to the whole piece or the whole set unless the numerator equals the denominator like $\frac{1}{1}$ or $\frac{2}{2}$ or $\frac{100}{100}$. Then you have a complete whole.

To review, a fraction has two numbers. One is high, and one is low. In between the numerator and the denominator is the dividing line. If we draw it like this, it may help you.

So the knife pointing down divides it, and the spatula facing up scoops it up. That's a way to always remember what each part means.

Now let's put it all together. The numerator goes on top, then the dividing line, and then the denominator. Fractions are closely related to division. In fact, one of the definitions of a fraction is a special form of division using a numerator and a denominator.

Okay. You know what the denominator and numerator means, but how do you say a fraction? Saying the numerator is no different than saying the number. With $\frac{1}{2}$ you say *one* for the numerator. With $\frac{3}{4}$ you say *three* for the numerator.

The denominator is a bit trickier, especially if you have trouble saying the "th" sound. It is not just saying the number. Here is a table that explains a bit more how to say the denominators.

Denominator	Example	How you say it?
2	$\frac{1}{2}$	One-half
3	$\frac{2}{3}$	Two-thirds
4	$\frac{3}{4}$	Three-fourths
5	$\frac{1}{5}$	One-fifth
from 6 on follow the pattern shown for 4 and 5	$\frac{2}{100}$	Two one-hundredths Add a "th" to the number. If the numerator is greater than one, add an "s" to the end of the "th."

You can see that once the denominator gets to four you add the "th" or the "ths" sound to the end of the number. Before that the denominators two and three are special cases.

So, using the table above, how would you say $\frac{1}{3}$ and $\frac{2}{5}$?

One-third and two-fifths.

Next, we know what the numerator and denominator mean by themselves, but what do they mean when they are working together?

Let's take two cans of soda. One can is divided into three parts, and Trusty gets $\frac{2}{3}$ of the can. The other can is divided into four parts, and Mayor Marbles gets $\frac{2}{4}$ of that can. How would you divide them?

The numerator of both fractions is two, but can you see that it's not the same amount of soda? Can you see that both

37

the numerator and denominator work together to tell how much of the whole we are talking about? The numerator and denominator only mean something in relationship to each other. The term for this is called *relativity*. It says that the top number means something only based on the value of the bottom number.

Now let's do a little hands-on fraction work that will help you understand fractions and how the numerator means something relative to the denominator.

Take a sheet of paper and fold it once so all the edges line up. Make a hamburger fold that gives you a wide piece instead of a hot dog fold that would give you a long piece. Now unfold it and look at it. You have two sections. How much is each section as part of the total?

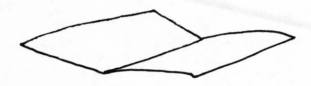

Now color in one-half of the paper.

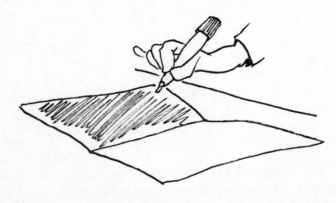

Now, take the same piece of paper, fold it back up in half, and fold it again. Then open it up. Now what fraction is each section?

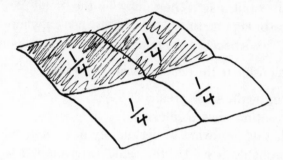

What fraction is the colored part of the whole? Notice that we have not colored any additional paper.

It is $\frac{2}{4}$.

PAUSE FOR THOUGHT

Fold the paper back up like it was and make another fold. Unfold it. What part of the whole is each section? What part of the whole is the colored section?

Each section is $\frac{1}{8}$ of the total. The colored section is $\frac{4}{8}$ of the whole paper.

Notice that we have never added any more color to the paper. It is still the same part of the paper that was colored in the beginning, but this time that part is called $\frac{4}{8}$.

Look back over all the paper foldings. After the first folding, the colored area was one section. After the second, the colored area was two sections. Then we moved to four sections, but each time it was the same area. The numerator kept getting bigger but it wasn't any more of the paper. That's because the numerator only means something in relationship to the denominator. The fractions $\frac{1}{2}$, $\frac{2}{4}$, and $\frac{4}{8}$ all describe the same area.

Wow, time passes quickly!

What do you want to bet that by now Dixie and Silver have probably arrived at the bank? How about if we take a break to see if even robbers use fractions?

Chapter 5
Mixin' Things Up

"Hear?" Silver whispered, his eyes sweeping the street, looking for innocent bystanders.

"They are arguing about who is going to get what part of the money, and something about a third key. They're waiting for the mayor to bring it," Dixie whispered back. "The robber is demanding to know why they need three keys."

Silver had read about the lock when it was first installed. "Special lock. Three keys. Three different people. Each unlocks a third of the mechanism. Supposed to be safer."

"I hope the mayor gets here soon," Dixie said with a shiver. "We need a plan."

Silver took a deep breath. He had to think fast.

"Good grief! Dixie sighed. "They are singing a math song."

"Singing?" Silver asked.

"Wait." Dixie tilted her head to the left. "I hear the mayor. He's just around the corner. Someone is with him."

Quickly Silver held out his hand, fingers splayed in a stop sign. The mayor pulled up so fast he almost spilled himself onto the sidewalk.

Silver motioned everyone toward him. He did have a plan, and with the mayor's help it might work.

So let's leave our superheroes and mayor to scheme, while we do a bit more with fractions.

You've learned about the basics. You know the difference between fractions and decimals, how both represent a part of the whole, and the parts of a fraction. Now, let's go a little deeper into the three different kinds of fractions: *proper fractions* (Sir P), *improper fractions* (Big I), and *mixed numbers* (Mr. M).

First, Sir P would tell you that with proper fractions the number on top is always smaller than the one underneath. With our new fraction lingo, we say the numerator is smaller than the denominator. In a math sentence we would write numerator < denominator.

The numerator always has to be smaller (but it doesn't have to be a lot smaller) for it to be a proper fraction.

For example, the fractions $\frac{2}{6}$, $\frac{4}{6}$, or $\frac{5}{6}$ are all still proper. But in each of these fractions, for them to be proper Max needs to be the denominator.

On a number line, proper fractions start with 0 and are less than one.

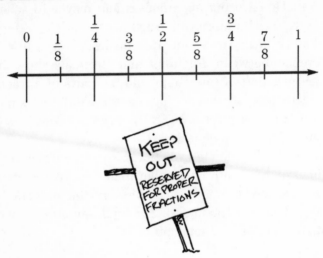

Since the numerator is always smaller than the denominator, it is always part of the whole. On this number line all the fractions we see are proper fractions. Any two numbers can be a proper fraction as long as the denominator is bigger than the numerator.

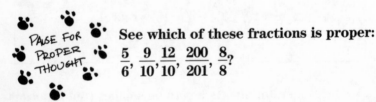

PAUSE FOR PROPER THOUGHT

See which of these fractions is proper:
$\frac{5}{6}$ $\frac{9}{10}$, $\frac{12}{10}$, $\frac{200}{201}$, $\frac{8}{8}$?

$\frac{5}{6}$, $\frac{9}{10}$, and $\frac{200}{201}$ are all proper fractions.

The fraction $\frac{12}{10}$ is called, as Big I would say, an improper fraction, and improper fractions turn proper fractions upside down. Mini and Max will again demonstrate.

While the proper fraction has a numerator that is smaller than the denominator, the improper fraction has a numerator that is equal to, or larger than, the denominator. In a math sentence you would write numerator ≥ denominator.

Improper fractions are top-heavy compared to proper fractions. They look like they could tip over any minute.

With a numerator that is greater than or equal to the denominator, on a number line improper fractions are not between zero and one.

They can start at one, go on toward two, and beyond. The one can be an improper fraction only if it's written as such. For example, $\frac{4}{4}$ and $\frac{5}{5}$ are both really just saying 1, but in an improper fraction way. Just like William and Bill are two names for the same person, $\frac{4}{4}$ and 1 are two names for the same amount.

Look at the number line below and name the improper fractions.

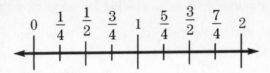

Here are a few more examples of improper, top-heavy fractions.

10/8 OF A PIZZA

$\frac{5}{4}$ OF A BONE

CHOP

4/3 OF A LOG

So you see, with $\frac{10}{8}$ of a pizza, you have one pizza and a bit more. With $\frac{5}{4}$ of a dog biscuit, you have one biscuit and a bit more. With $\frac{4}{3}$ of a log, you have one log and a great chance to roast marshmallows.

Finally, last, but certainly not least, Mr. M wants you to know about mixed numbers. Mixed numbers are on the number line after one. They are a combination of two different types of numbers: a mix of a proper fraction and a whole number. With a mix, the first part of the number is a whole number, like a whole mango or a whole dog bone. A whole of anything is complete. It hasn't been divided into any parts, or if it has been divided, the parts are all present and accounted for. And the number that describes that whole is called:

A WHOLE NUMBER

So the first part of the mixed fraction $2\frac{1}{4}$ is the whole number two. The second part is the proper fraction $\frac{1}{4}$. Mathematicians were too lazy to write $2 + \frac{1}{4}$ all the time so they just put the two numbers together. But really $2\frac{1}{4}$ means $2 + \frac{1}{4}$.

And now here come Mini and Max to demo this concept even further. Look who they have brought with them.

Mixed numbers are like improper fractions on the number line. Since they have the whole with them, they are after the one, but they do not include one.

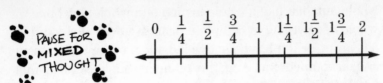

Number line: 0, $\frac{1}{4}$, $\frac{1}{2}$, $\frac{3}{4}$, 1, $1\frac{1}{4}$, $1\frac{1}{2}$, $1\frac{3}{4}$, 2

What are the mixed numbers on this number line?

$1\frac{1}{4}, 1\frac{1}{2},$ and $1\frac{3}{4}$

Notice that the other fractions: $\frac{1}{4}$, $\frac{1}{2}$, and $\frac{3}{4}$ aren't mixed numbers because they don't include a whole number.

Now that you know all three kinds of fractions—proper fractions, improper fractions, and mixed numbers—listen in on the robbers at the bank.

I GET $1\frac{3}{4}$ OF THE MONEY

DO YOUR PART MR. M

I'M TAKING 4/3 OF THE MONEY.

I'M TAKING 4/5 OF THE MONEY BECAUSE YOU TWO ONLY SHARE $\frac{1}{5}$ OF THE BRAINS

What is wrong with this picture? (*Hint:* Big I and Mr. M are definitely off in their knowledge of fractions.)

Big I and Mr. M both say they are taking more than the whole vault of money. Both $\frac{3}{4}$ and $1\frac{3}{4}$ are more than the whole amount in the vault because they are both after one on the number line.

48

Right! Two of the types of fractions have something in common. They both are talking about the same amounts in a different way. The question is, can improper fractions and mixed numbers be changed back and forth? If you understand what they mean, it's easy to see that they can.

One way to convert improper fractions to mixed numbers is to draw a picture. For example, take the improper fraction $\frac{17}{8}$ of a pizza. You know by looking at the denominator that each pizza was divided into eight pieces. So you draw the first pizza with eight pieces and a second pizza with eight pieces.

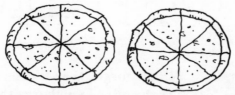

8 PIECES + 8 PIECES. IS THAT ENOUGH?

Not quite. It's only sixteen pieces so far. So you know you need one more of the next pizza which is still divided into eight pieces.

So $\frac{17}{8}$ is

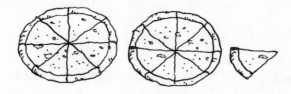

And the above picture is how you represent the improper fraction $\frac{17}{8}$.

49

Now, using this same picture, how would you convert that fraction to a mixed number? Remember, a mixed number is a combination of a whole number and a proper fraction.

Don't forget that the second part of the mixed number is the proper fraction. So the next question is, how many parts of a pizza do you have?

$$\frac{8}{1}$$

Now put it all together: two whole pizzas and $\frac{1}{8}$ of a part of pizza = $2\frac{1}{8}$. So the improper fraction $\frac{17}{8}$ = the mixed number $2\frac{1}{8}$. That's how you convert it if you want to draw a picture, but there is a way to do it without drawing a picture.

Dixie has put it all together into one quick list:

— INSTRUCTIONS —

1. DIVIDE THE NUMERATOR BY THE DENOMINATOR. THE QUESTION IS HOW MANY WHOLES DO YOU HAVE?

2. WRITE DOWN THE WHOLE NUMBER ANSWER.

3. ASK HOW MUCH IS LEFT AFTER THE NUMERATOR IS DIVIDED BY THE DENOMINATOR. PUT THAT NUMBER OVER THE DENOMINATOR.

4. PUT THE WHOLE NUMBER WITH THE PROPER FRACTION.

Let's see how it works. Take the improper fraction $\frac{23}{9}$.

1. Divide the numerator by the denominator: $23 \div 9 = 2$.
2. The whole number is 2.
3. How much was left over when you divided? $9 \times 2 = 18$. So $23 - 18 = 5$ left over, and that goes over the denominator to make $\frac{5}{9}$.

4. Putting it all together gives you $2\frac{5}{9}$.

You try. What would $\frac{8}{6}$ be as a mixed number? Use the steps and try it yourself.

(In the next chapter, we will learn how to simplify this mixed fraction to $1\frac{1}{3}$).

Step 1: $8 \div 6 = 1$. Step 2: Write down 1. Step 3: Remainder is 2, so put it over the denominator to get $\frac{2}{6}$. Step 4: Put both parts together to get $1\frac{2}{6}$.

Of course, mixed numbers can also be converted to improper fractions. Let's say Dixie made $3\frac{1}{2}$ sweet potato pies for this demonstration. She wants Mayor Marbles and Mongrel to figure out what the improper fraction would be so she can figure out how many $\frac{1}{2}$ pieces she has. Then she will know to how many people she can give a $\frac{1}{2}$ of a piece of pie.

First draw three pies, and then $\frac{1}{2}$ of a pie. Note that all the pies need to be cut in two pieces like the denominator says.

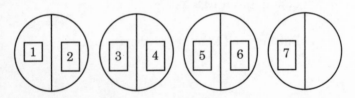

Now count the $\frac{1}{2}$ pieces. You get seven pieces so the improper fraction for $3\frac{1}{2}$ is $\frac{7}{2}$.

That's how you convert mixed numbers to improper fractions by drawing it out, but there is a way to do it without the pictures.

Here's a trick to help you remember the steps visually.

$$3\frac{1}{2}$$

It means first take 2×3, and then add the one. Put that solution over the denominator of two. So $3\frac{1}{2} = \frac{7}{2}$.

Here are the steps in writing:

- – INSTRUCTIONS –
1. MULTIPLY THE WHOLE NUMBER PART BY THE FRACTION'S DENOMINATOR.
2. ADD BOTH NUMERATORS TOGETHER: THE NUMERATOR FROM THE WHOLES AND THE NUMERATOR THAT IS PART OF THE PROPER FRACTION.
3. WRITE THE RESULTS ON TOP OF THE DENOMINATOR

Now you try. What would $2\frac{3}{5}$ be as an improper fraction?

Step 1: $2 \times 5 = 10$. Step 2: Put the numerators together $10 + 3 = 13$. Step 3: Put the numerator from Step 2 over the denominator $\frac{13}{5}$.

See? The different types of fractions are easy to understand. So let's go back to our superheroes.

"Can you do this?" Silver whispered to Mayor Marbles.

The mayor pulled himself up proudly. "Absolutely," he replied softly. "I'd do anything to save my town."

Trusty looked rather doubtful, but Silver just nodded. He just hoped the mayor could carry out his third of the plan.

Mayor Marbles took a deep breath, let it out, and stepped in front of the door.

"It took you long enough," Big I said, stepping aside so Mayor Marbles could pass by.

Without so much as a BLAM, Dixie popped out from behind the mayor and punched Big I out with her strong right hand. He went down with a whoosh—his eyes filling with Daring Dots—Dixie ducked, pulling Mayor Marbles down with her.

Controlling his mind and his body, Silver did what he did best. One leg extended, the other bent at the knee, one arm outstretched, the other bent at the elbow, he flew over the mayor and Dixie like Jackie Chan.

And the fight was on.

"Silver. I think we have a problem," Dixie said, getting up. She nodded toward Sir P holding the bank manager hostage with his gentleman's cane. She took a brownie from her pocket, and then, with slow precision, began to unwrap the treat.

Chapter 6
Searching for Equals

"Dear lady, slide me the key," Sir P insisted, poking his cane into the bank manager's ribs. "Quickly."

"Do what he asks," Dixie said. She took the key from the mayor and advanced toward the robber, licking brownie crumbs off her fingers.

"Dear Madame!" the robber said. "Germs are passed that way. It's very unhygienic."

"I thought you'd be hungry," Dixie said, holding up the brownie, waving it back and forth in front of his eyes.

She took another step forward.

"It smells scrumptious," Sir P said, "but I wouldn't eat anything that touched licked fingers. Forget the goodies. Give me the key."

"Okay," Dixie said in a soothing tone. "If you want the key, you can have the key," and with a sweeping motion she slid it across the floor.

"Thank you," Sir P said, bending down to pick it up. He plucked a silk handkerchief from his pocket, wiped off the germs, and inserted the third key into the lock. Then he gave one twist to the right.

Suddenly the screen by the keypad came to life. The words, "Equivalent to one key, in the set of three. A fraction that's its equal, it must be," scrolled across the screen.

"What's this?" asked Sir P.

"A math riddle. After all we do live in Mathopolis," said the bank manager.

Looking smug, Sir P typed in a number. The motor of the automatic opener hummed to life, and the heavy door began to swing out.

Knowing equivalent fractions helped Sir P, it also will help you.

Equivalent is a big word, but it's not hard. When it's all chopped up it simply means "equal." If you looked at equivalent fractions on the number line you would see that all equivalent fractions share the same exact spot.

Remember the paper folding in Chapter 4? You shaded an area and kept folding. Although the shaded area never changed, the way you talked about it did.

While the section was divided into a different number of pieces, the area shaded didn't vary. That's because $\frac{1}{2}$ and $\frac{2}{4}$ and $\frac{4}{8}$ are equivalent fractions. They are all equal. In a math statement you would write $\frac{1}{2} = \frac{2}{4} = \frac{4}{8}$.

Making equivalent fractions involves dividing things up or gluing parts back together.

You can handle this mathematically by doing the same thing to both the numerator and denominator. As long as you are either dividing or multiplying both the numerator and denominator by the same number.

It's that simple.

If you multiply the numerator and denominator by the same number you make the number more *complex*. For example, multiplying the numerator and denominator of the fraction $\frac{2}{4}$ by two gives you $\frac{4}{8}$.

Dividing both the numerator and denominator by two gives you $\frac{1}{2}$. The process of dividing $\frac{2}{4}$ to make the fraction $\frac{1}{2}$ is called *simplifying* a fraction, and this is a great math skill.

To simplify means to make the fraction less complicated, like gluing parts of a fraction back together, and to get simplified fractions, you divide both the numerator and denominator by the same number. The question is: What number?

For this we go to an agent in the Fraction Secret Service.

Let's take a closer look by taking his name apart. Greatest Common Factor, or GFC, is made up of three words. Let's look at the most difficult word first: *factor*.

You can think of factors as partners, not partners in crime, but partners in multiplication.

If you are finding the factors of six, while two is one factor, it can do nothing without its partner in multiplication—three.

Factors of any given number represent all the different ways you arrive at that number by multiplying two whole numbers together. Want to find the factors of the number eight? Ask yourself, how can you make eight by multiplying?

The last two multiplication facts are copycats of the first two, so the factors of eight are 1, 2, 4, and 8.

You can also think of factors as all the different ways to group a number of objects, like Mongrel did with the factors for six.

Finally, another way to think of factors is using rectangles and area. If you want to find the factors of eight, make a rectangle with the area of eight using only whole numbers.

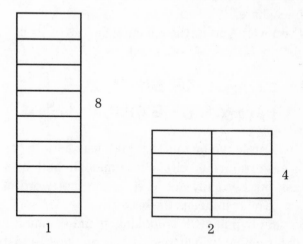

The second word in GCF is *common*. People can have friends in common, ride a common bus, or even share common germs.

AHHHHH CHOO!

With GCF, common talks about the *factors* two or more numbers share.

If you were finding the common factors of six and eight, first list the factors of both numbers.

FACTORS OF SIX: 1, 2, 3, 6
FACTORS OF EIGHT: 1, 2, 4, 8

Next, circle the factors that both lists have in common. In this case you would circle the 1 and 2 in both lists.

Last, but certainly not least, is the first word of GCF, *greatest*. Greatest means the biggest.

So simply put, GCF is looking at the common factors and determining which one is the greatest, and two is definitely better than one.

The factors of six and eight may be easy, but what if you need to find the factors of twenty-four and thirty-six? How can you possibly find them all?

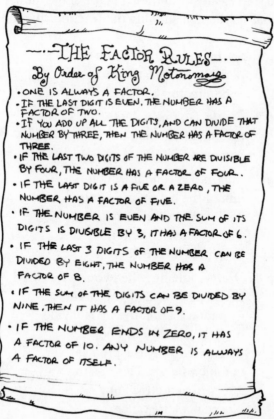

There is one more work-saving secret, and that is no matter how hard you try, some numbers don't have factors other than one and themselves. These are called *prime numbers*. So if you see these numbers, don't bother trying to search for other factors: 2, 3, 5, 7, 11, 13, 17, 19. These are the smaller prime numbers.

Now you have the tips for finding factors from GCF, but do you remember why you are finding factors?

To make equal fractions, you have to divide or multiply the numerator and denominator by the same number. When you find the Greatest Common Factor of the numerator and denominator, you can simplify the fraction. Just do this:

Step 1. *Search.* Find the factors of both the numerator and denominator.

Step 2. *Circle.* Go through the list and circle all the common factors.

Step 3. *Award.* Determine which one of the common factors is the greatest, and award it the Greatest Common Factor award (GCF).

Step 4. *Divide.* Finally, when you've followed the steps of finding the Greatest Common Factor, then you divide both the numerator and denominator by the greatest common factor. This has the affect of actually gluing pieces back together.

Let's look at an example. Take the number $\frac{5}{10}$.

Step 1 is a factor search of both the numerator and denominator. To do this you need to use the scroll, your multiplication table, and the prime number list.

Step 2 is to circle all the common factors.

Step 3 is to determine which of the common factors is greatest and give it the award.

Finally, *Step 4* is to divide both the numerator and the denominator by five.

Now it's time to work with a difficult fraction like $\frac{36}{24}$. Remember, all the helpful hints you need to juggle in your head? Well, now we are going to add one more.

First, we need to find the factors of thirty-six. If you use the king's list and your multiplication tables you find the numbers: 1, 2, 3, 4, 6, 9, and 36. But you know some are missing. That's where your new skill comes in.

Remember, every number has a partner in multiplication.

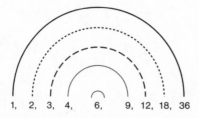

How can you make sure that each factor has its partner? The answer is, ta-da, the factor rainbow.

1, 2, 3, 4, 6, 9, 12, 18, 36

Each factor is connected to its partner by the arc of a rainbow.

One has an arc of a rainbow that connects it to thirty-six. They are partner-factors that make thirty-six.

67

Two has an arc of a rainbow connecting it to eighteen. They are partner-factors that make thirty-six.

The rainbow arc gets smaller and smaller until the two numbers next to each other are joined by an arc, or the number is joined to itself as in the case of six. In this case, six is called a *twin*. A twin is multiplied by itself to get thirty-six.

Now you find the factors of twenty-four.

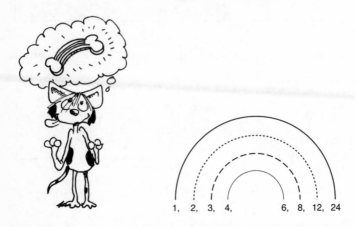

1, 2, 3, 4, 6, 8, 12, 24

Next circle the common factors of thirty-six and twenty-four.

Factors of 36 are ①, ②, ③, ④, ⑥, 9, ⑫, 18, 36.
Factors of 24 are ①, ②, ③, ④, ⑥, 8, ⑫, 24.

Which number gets the Greatest Common Factor award?

Finally, use the GCF to simplify the fraction.

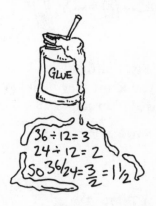

$36 \div 12 = 3$
$24 \div 12 = 2$
So $36/24 = \frac{3}{2} = 1\frac{1}{2}$

And, there is one more thing about simplifying. What if you find a factor, but not the greatest one? Like the problem $\frac{100}{250}$? What if you don't know the list of factors, but you do know that ten goes into both numbers (because they both end in zero)?

Pretend you are carrying the numbers down a ladder. The first rung of the ladder is to divide both the numerator and denominator by ten and get $\frac{10}{25}$.

Can you simplify it further? Yes, because they both end in a zero or five you know they both have a factor of 5, so divide both by five. For example, $10 \div 5 = 2$, and $25 \div 5 = 5$, so the next rung down is $\frac{2}{5}$.

Now it's your turn. Here are a few simplifying problems.

Simplify each of the following fractions: $\frac{12}{48}$, $\frac{49}{14}$, **and** $3\frac{15}{25}$. **You can use either the GCF fraction agent or the ladder rung technique.**

from Chapter 5), $3\frac{15}{25} = 3\frac{3}{5}$

$\frac{12}{48} = \frac{1}{4}$, $\frac{49}{14} = \frac{7}{2}$ or $3\frac{1}{2}$ (using your knowledge

Sir P opened the vault by knowing something about equivalent fractions himself. He answered the riddle by making a fraction that was equivalent to $\frac{1}{3}$. He entered $\frac{2}{6}$, and presto, he mastered the lock. The money was out in the open.

"Help me," the bank manager cried, pushing against the massive steel door with his shoulder. "We have to close it."

The door didn't budge.

"Excuse me," Sir P said, "but you are ruining my bank robbery." He poked his cane hard into the bank manager's side.

"You're hurting him," Egweena cried, stepping forward.

"Please, back up," Sir P said, waving his cane toward the children.

Egweena stopped. "Dixie! Do something!"

Dixie took a slow step forward, still offering the brownie.

All heads turned to look at the tied-up, drooling criminals. It was the distraction Silver needed.

"Well," Mayor Marbles said, dusting himself off. "That was exciting."

"Children," Mr. Little said as he clapped his hands three times. "We need to be going now. Let's line up."

"In a minute," Sticky called, putting both hands on the vault door. "Come on!"

"You know," Mayor Marbles said, absentmindedly sticking his head in the vault. "I don't think I've ever seen inside one of these."

"Thank you," the bank manager said. "I feel much better now, don't you, Mayor Marbles?"

Everyone looked around.

"Mayor Marbles?" Trusty called. "Has anyone seen the mayor?"

Dixie looked around the room. "Mayor Marbles? Where is—"

"In there," Egweena answered, pointing toward the vault. A collective gasp filled the room as everyone turned to look.

The keys were gone.

Chapter 7
It's Not Easy Being Common

"I can't believe the mayor was in the vault when we closed the door," the bank manager said, rubbing his forehead with his fingers.

"Will he be okay?" Trusty asked anxiously.

"The vault is designed like a safe house," the bank manager explained. "He has plenty of air and water, but that's it—no bed, TV, chairs, computer, and worst yet, no food. We need to get him out."

"No hamburgers. Fries," Silver said in a low, sad voice as he scratched Mongrel behind the ears.

"Focus," Dixie said, thumping Silver on the arm. It was annoying how he always thought of food.

Silver shook himself out of his imagination and said, "Find keys."

"Yes. You must," the bank manager said. "Not only for the mayor's sake, but whoever has the keys could take all the town's money!"

"Oh, my," Dixie said wondering where to start. She scanned the room for anything that seemed out of place.

"Strange! Looks like whoever left this doesn't like fractions," Dixie said, showing the paper she found to Silver. "I wonder—"

"Fingerprint," he said, taking the page and folding it carefully before slipping it into his pocket. "After radio station."

Mongrel howled in agreement.

"Okay. You drive, and I'll listen for clues," she said. "We need to find those keys, but where could they be?"

Where indeed!

Poor Mayor Marbles has really gotten himself into a jam this time, and not the kind with peanut butter! But while the superheroes search for the keys, you can learn how to do another type of search.

PAUSE FOR
GLUING OR
CHOPPING

Before you begin let's do a quick review. Do you remember how to simplify a fraction by using the fraction agent with the code named GCF? Do you chop or glue? Do you divide or multiply?

Simplifying is gluing and dividing.

If you are making equivalent fractions, but you aren't simplifying them, you are making them more complex. Why? Because you are trying to get more than one fraction to have the same denominator before you compare or order, add or subtract. What's the best denominator for the job? To find this you need to meet the Least Common Multiple.

Like the GCF agent you met in the last chapter, LCM's mission is also making equivalent fractions, but his job is to make denominators the same when you are working with more than one fraction.

LCM's real name is Least Common Multiple. Again, since this is a book about fractions, let's take the name, *Least Common Multiple*, apart.

Let's start with the hardest word: *multiple*. A multiple is what you get when you multiply. You can think of multiples as the answers, or products, in your multiplication table. If you want to find the multiples of two, they are the products for each time you multiply two times another number. For 2×2, the multiple would be four. The multiples of two are 0, 2, 4, 6, 8, 10, 12, 14, and they go on and on. (Although zero is a multiple, it can't be used as a denominator.)

The second word, *common*, is the way agent GCF and LCM are identical. In this case, it means the multiples that two or more numbers have in common, or share.

The first word, *least*, is easy. As Mr. Little's students would say it means, "least," "tiniest," "flea-size," and "amoeba-like."

It's LCM's job to find the Least Common Multiple of more than one fraction's denominator and make that LCM the new denominator.

So how does LCM do its job? Think of finding the Least Common Multiple of more than one denominator as finding the connection between two people who have been charged with a crime.

They act like they don't know each other. They look nothing alike, but if you work hard enough, you will find something they have in common. Multiples are the same thing.

Let's see how it works when dealing with fractions.

Wait! Are Fraction Secret Service agents dancing in your head? Not to worry. We are now going to see secret files of GCF and LCM, but before you look, you must promise not to share this information. These are some of the trickiest and best secret agents the Fraction Secret Service has. Their identity must be protected.

I PROMISE

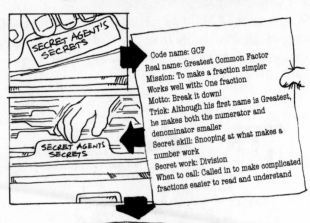

Code name: GCF
Real name: Greatest Common Factor
Mission: To make a fraction simpler
Works well with: One fraction
Motto: Break it down!
Trick: Although his first name is Greatest, he makes both the numerator and denominator smaller
Secret skill: Snooping at what makes a number work
Secret work: Division
When to call: Called in to make complicated fractions easier to read and understand

Code name: LCM
Real name: Least Common Multiple
Mission: To find the Least Common denominator for making equivalent fractions
Works well with: Two or more fractions that need a common denominator so they can be compared, ordered, added, or subtracted
Motto: Build it up!
Trick: Has the name Least but often makes both the numerator and denominator greater
Secret skill: Finding the relatives of a denominator
Secret work: Multiplication
When to call: Called in at the beginning of mission when comparing, ordering, adding and subtracting
Special Assignment: Watch out for zero who is always trying to sneak in to become a denominator.

As we begin to work with Agent LCM, things will become clearer, so let's start with the fractions $\frac{5}{12}$, $\frac{9}{24}$, and $\frac{3}{2}$. How can we make their denominators common?

The answer is to find a relative they all have in common. In math talk that means finding a common multiple.

One approach is to list the multiples in the form of a table. First, list multiples of each denominator of $\frac{5}{12}$, $\frac{9}{24}$, and $\frac{3}{2}$ by multiplying the denominator by the numbers one, two, three, and so on. (Remember zero is disqualified from the competition.) If you do these lists in a table, it is easy to see what you are doing.

Secret Agent Table												
Number	1	2	3	4	5	6	7	8	9	10	11	12
Multiples of 2	2	4	6	8	10	12	14	16	18	20	22	24
Multiples of 12	12	24										
Multiples of 24	24											

The first row lists the numbers used in multiplying, the second row lists all the multiples of the denominator two, the third row lists all the multiples of twelve, and the fourth row lists the multiples of twenty-four.

When you make this table, stop when you find one common multiple in all three rows. This will save you a lot of work. In this case you stopped with 24, which was common in all the multiple rows.

So the least common multiple of the denominators of $\frac{5}{12}$, $\frac{9}{24}$, and $\frac{3}{2}$ is 24. Now you try one. Fine the LCM of $\frac{1}{2}$, $\frac{2}{3}$, and $\frac{1}{4}$.

Remember, first make a table.

Okay, now fill in the table. Try to do it quickly and remember, stop when you find a common multiple.

Did you get the right answer?

Number	1	2	3	4	5	6
Multiples of 2	2	4	6	8	10	12
Multiples of 3	3	6	9	12		
Multiples of 4	4	8	12			

Now search the lists and find the common denominator. Quick! What did you get?

12

Great job! You've solved the problem!

When finding the common denominator of fractions, using a table to determine a common multiple is often a good place to start. But if you can't find one easily by using a table, there are other ways to approach the problem.

One way is to not worry about whether it is the LCM of the denominator. You just make it common. You can do that by multiplying both or all the denominators together.

For example, say you have $\frac{1}{5}$ and $\frac{2}{8}$ and you don't know what the common denominator is. You can simply multiply $5 \times 8 = 40$ and make 40 the denominator. That way you know you have a denominator that is common. You don't know, though, if it's the least, or lowest.

Now, let's open up some case files and see if there are any problems you can solve.

CASE FILES

YOUR MISSION SHOULD YOU CHOOSE TO ACCEPT IT, IS TO FIND THE LCM OF THE DENOMINATOR FOR THE FOLLOWING FRACTIONS:

1. 3/4 AND 2/5
2. 5/9 AND 1/3
3. 3/4 AND 1/2
4. AND FINALLY SOLVE THE PROBLEM THAT MAY BE A CLUE AT THE BEGINNING OF THE CHAPTER. WHAT DO THE FRACTIONS 1/6, 5/12 AND 7/9 HAVE IN COMMON?

Okay. Let's see if you have earned your rank of Advanced Agent!

1.

Number	1	2	3	4	5	6
Multiples of 4	4	8	12	16	20	
Multiples of 5	5	10	15	20		

LCM is 20.

2.

Number	1	2	3	4
Multiples of 3	3	6	9	
Multiples of 9	9			

LCM is 9.

3.

Number	1	2	3
Multiples of 2	2	4	
Multiples of 4	4		

LCM is 4.

4.

Number	1	2	3	4	5	6
Multiples of 6	6	12	18	24	30	36
Multiples of 9	9	18	27	36		
Multiples of 12	12	24	36			

LCM is 36.

See? Finding the Least Common Multiple is a lot easier than getting poor Mayor Marbles out of the vault or finding the keys.

So let's head back to Mathopolis to see if any new clues have surfaced.

Silver glanced at Dixie. Her intensity when she was listening sometimes surprised him.

"Hear?" he asked, turning right toward the back of the bank.

"Nothing," Dixie said, settling back against the seat. "But bank keys don't disappear into thin air."

Two armed guards stood outside the bank, guarding the perimeter. They waved as Dixie and Silver passed by.

"It's good Mary Martha could work you into her radio show on such short notice," Dixie said, pushing the button to close the window. "You can ask the people of Mathopolis to keep their eyes open."

And while the superheroes make their way to the radio station, let's look in and see what's up with Shabang.

Chapter 8
Out of Order

How did the keys get here? She wondered, pulling up her stocking and smoothing away the wrinkles in her skirt. She couldn't remember. It was like she'd developed a fuzzy place inside her mind and time sometimes disappeared. She lost a minute or so when the kids were playing The Flying Dutchman the other day. One minute Egweena and her partner were running the circle, and the next thing Shabang knew, she was doing a ballet dance.

And then there was the time when Mr. Little had written the fractions on the board and asked the kids to put them in order. One minute she had been standing at his side looking at the fractions $\frac{2}{5}$, $\frac{1}{3}$, and $\frac{4}{15}$, and the next he was scolding her.

"Ms. Shabang, I wasn't done with the problem," he had said.

She'd looked down at the eraser in her hand and then saw the problem was gone from the board.

"Tidiness is very important," she'd said, but she wasn't sure what she had done or why.

It creeped her out!

And now this!

The three bank keys were here, on her bed, and she had no idea why. Had *she* taken them? Surely not!

Maybe the bank manager asked her to watch them for some reason. It would come to her.

She walked out to the living room and turned on the radio. Television was too chaotic, with all the commercials splitting apart the story. Satellite radio suited her just fine. "Silver, can you tell us what happened at the bank?" the reporter was saying.

"Robbed. Mayor locked in vault. Keys missing." Silver said. "Help."

"Okay. There you have it," the reporter babbled on. "Mayor Marbles is locked in the bank vault, and the three special keys to unlock the vault are missing. If anyone knows anything—"

"Keys?" Shabang cried out loud. What was going on?

She hurried into the bedroom and stared at the keys. What if someone saw them? Told the police? She'd be arrested.

She grabbed a pillowcase off the bed and stuffed the three keys inside. She had to help the mayor; she had to take the keys back so the vault could be opened.

She grabbed the pillowcase, tucked it under her arm, and stopped. Sweat broke out on her forehead. If she did that, the keys would be split apart. Three people would take one key. The group would be broken into thirds. That wasn't right. Only she couldn't think about that now. She had to help the mayor. He'd been in the vault now all day, and he was so hungry!

Suddenly she froze, then slowly brought her feet into the fifth ballet position. Her hair sprang from its tight bun, and the bag of keys slipped to the floor.

Wow! Have you ever been in a crazy situation like Shabang's? Only in your situation you needed to compare fractions?

To answer this you need to compare or order fractions. Sometimes fractions are as easy to compare and order as whole numbers, and sometimes they are not. These would be fractions that have one number in common.

Pretend you are on a game show, and this is your million-dollar question: "What part of a fraction needs to be the same to make comparison easy?" Your choices are: the numerator, the denominator, or the whole number? You want to go home with the cash. You think hard.

Both the denominator and the numerator are the answers. If you picked the whole number go back to the beginning of the book—do not pass GO and do not collect $200.

If you have mixed numbers, and the whole numbers are the same, it makes it harder to compare. But having the same numerator or denominator helps.

Let's start by looking at fractions that have the same numerator.

Numerators are the same

Say your friend is sick of his Halloween candy. He has forty pieces left, and he asks, "Would you rather have $\frac{1}{2}$, $\frac{1}{4}$, or

$\frac{1}{8}$?" Notice the numerators are the same. What would you answer if you wanted as much as possible?

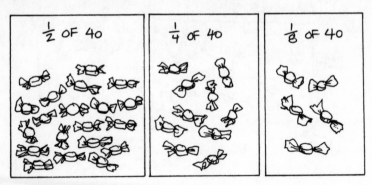

When the numerators are the same, the fractions get smaller when the denominator gets bigger. Here's another way to look at it. Take one piece of candy and divide it up in three ways. In each, only shade one part because the numerator is always one.

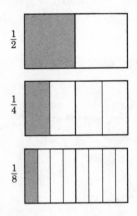

A bigger denominator means it's divided into more parts. So $\frac{1}{8} < \frac{1}{4} < \frac{1}{2}$.

When the numerators are the same, a bigger denominator makes the fractions smaller. So if you wanted a lot of candy, you would have answered $\frac{1}{2}$.

What if you compared $\frac{2}{3}$, $\frac{2}{8}$, and $\frac{2}{5}$? Which fraction is the smallest? Which is the biggest?

$\frac{2}{8}$ is the smallest, and $\frac{2}{3}$ is the biggest. $\frac{2}{5}$ is in the middle. In a math sentence it would look like $\frac{2}{3} > \frac{2}{5} > \frac{2}{8}$, or $\frac{2}{8} < \frac{2}{5} < \frac{2}{3}$.

Now let's take a look at some fractions with the same denominators.

Denominators

When the denominators are the same, ask yourself how many ninths each fraction has. Then see if you can put them in order using a math sentence.

Easy, right? When you are comparing fractions with the same denominator, the value and order is determined by the numerator.

Fractions with mixed numbers can also be easy to compare if their whole numbers are different.

If you were Sticky, how much homework would you rather have, $2\frac{2}{3}$ pages, $1\frac{1}{2}$ pages, or $3\frac{3}{4}$ pages? When the whole numbers are different, you can ignore the fraction when comparing. (If there is an improper fraction, you must make it a mixed number first to compare.) You know that one is less than two which is less than three, so it makes sense to think that $1\frac{1}{2}$ is less than $2\frac{2}{3}$ which is less than $3\frac{3}{4}$. In a math sentence it looks like: $1 < 2 < 3$, so you know that $1\frac{1}{2} < 2\frac{2}{3} < 3\frac{3}{4}$. Sticky would definitely rather have $1\frac{1}{2}$ pages of homework.

So far you've compared fractions with the same numerators, fractions with the same denominators, and mixed numbers with different whole numbers. Now, let's move on to harder stuff. When both denominators and numerators are different, it's hard to tell which fractions are larger.

One way to compare them is to use a number line and benchmark fractions. These are famous fractions, fractions that most people are familiar with.

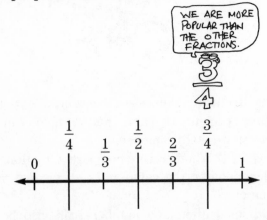

Say Mr. Little took a survey of where his students want to go on the next field trip. Option A, which was a peaceful nursery, got $\frac{3}{8}$ of the vote. Option B, which was a jail, got $\frac{1}{3}$

of the vote. The rest of the students wanted to avoid the danger and stay at school so they didn't vote. You can use the number line to figure out which option got the most votes. Estimate where each fraction goes on the number line.

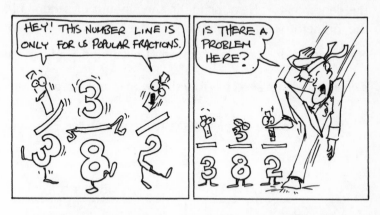

Yes, $\frac{3}{8}$ belongs between $\frac{1}{3}$ and $\frac{1}{2}$ because $\frac{3}{8}$ is less than $\frac{1}{2}$ but more than $\frac{1}{3}$. It's $\frac{1}{8}$ less than $\frac{4}{8}$, which is equivalent to $\frac{1}{2}$. And it is a bit more than $\frac{3}{9}$ which is equivalent to $\frac{1}{3}$. It was easy for $\frac{1}{3}$, since it's already a popular fraction.

Now, look at the number line, compare $\frac{3}{8}$ and $\frac{1}{2}$. Which one is greater? Notice that the fractions get bigger as you move to the right.

$\frac{1}{3} < \frac{3}{8}$ so the nursery got more votes than the jail.

Great job! Benchmark fractions can help you compare a lot of fractions.

Another approach for comparing fractions, still using a picture, is to divide a rectangle into as many pieces as are in the denominator. Next, shade in the amount of sections in the numerator. Do a picture for each fraction you are comparing. For example, if mouse #1 has found $\frac{2}{3}$ of a piece a cheese and mouse #2 has found $\frac{5}{6}$, who found more cheese?

If you compare the pictures visually you can see $\frac{5}{6}$ is more than $\frac{2}{3}$.

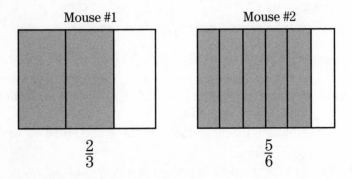

But what if the fractions are too complicated to use benchmarks or pictures? The answer is to change the fractions, presto chango.

You've learned about changing the look of fractions by making equivalent fractions. To do this you multiplied or divided both the numerator and denominator by the same number.

Now the question is, what do you change the fractions into to make them easier to compare? You already know that fractions are easier to compare when they share the same numerator or denominator. But, since changing the numerators changes the value of the fraction, the denominator has to be the one to morph.

To compare fractions like $\dfrac{5}{12}$ and $\dfrac{9}{24}$ and $\dfrac{3}{2}$ you have to get a common denominator. So what fraction secret agent can help?

You've already learned the first half of the mission of making equivalent fractions in Chapter 7: finding the Least Common Multiple of the denominator. Do you remember how you used the Secret Agent Table and then Stop for common multiples?

After you figure out the common denominator, your mission, should you choose to accept it, is to learn the next step, called the Disguise, and to make each fraction into a new equivalent fraction.

All the fractions will have to change to the denominator picked as the LCM. They will still be the same fraction, but they will look very different.

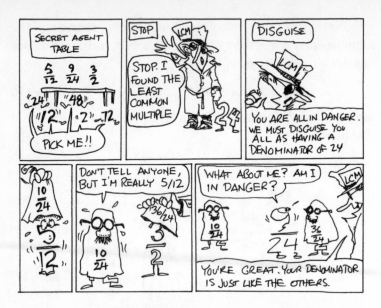

Now let's use the three stages—Secret Agent Table, Stop, and Disguise—to figure out what the fractions $\frac{1}{2}$, $\frac{7}{6}$, and $\frac{5}{8}$ have for a common denominator, and make the appropriate changes.

Start with the table technique to find the Least Common Multiple.

Secret Agent Table												
Number	1	2	3	4	5	6	7	8	9	10	11	12
Multiples of 2	2	4	6	8	10	12	14	16	18	20	22	24
Multiples of 6	6	12	18	24								
Multiples of 8	8	16	24									

Do you see any number that is in all the rows? Stop when you find it. That's the least common denominator.

If you picked twenty-four for your denominator, you are right. And while the mission may seem nearly done, it's not. Each fraction now has to be transformed into a new fraction with a denominator of twenty-four. Remember the numerators and denominators will get mad if they aren't treated fairly.

First, disguise $\frac{1}{2}$.

Look at your table. You'll see you multiplied 2 by 12 to get 24. To keep the fraction equivalent, you need to multiply $1 \times 12 = 12$, which gives us the equivalent fraction of $\frac{12}{24}$.

Try it yourself. Repeat the process and change the other fractions of $\frac{7}{6}$ and $\frac{5}{8}$ so that they have the common denominator of 24.

First disguise $\frac{7}{6}$ so it has a denominator of 24. What did you multiply 6 by to get 24?

LOOK AT YOUR TABLE AND FIND THE 24 IN THE ROW OF MULTIPLES OF SIX. WHAT COLUMN IS IT IN?

The answer is four.

Next, multiply the numerator by the same number that you multiplied the denominator by.

$$\frac{7 \times 4}{6 \times 4} = \frac{28}{24}$$

So $\frac{7}{6} = \frac{28}{24}$.

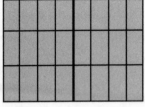 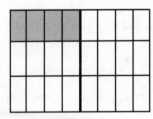

$$\frac{7}{6} = \frac{28}{24}$$

Now for $\frac{5}{8}$. Disguise $\frac{5}{8}$ so it has a denominator of 24. What did you multiply 8 by to get 24? Again, look at your table.

The answer is three.

So multiply the numerator by the same number that you multiplied the denominator by.

$$\frac{5 \times 3}{8 \times 3} = \frac{15}{24}$$

So $\frac{5}{8} = \frac{15}{24}$.

Finally! Now with all the fractions having the same denominator, you can compare and order them. What is the proper order for $\frac{1}{2} = \frac{12}{24}$, $\frac{7}{6} = \frac{28}{24}$, and $\frac{5}{8} = \frac{15}{24}$?

$\frac{12}{24}, \frac{15}{24},$ and finally $\frac{28}{24}.$ In a math sentence, we would write: $\frac{12}{24} > \frac{15}{24} > \frac{28}{24}.$

Try one by yourself. Use the LCM agent for changing the denominators. Remember Shabang saying that Mr. Little fussed at her once because she erased some fractions? Well, let's compare and order those fractions that she erased: $\frac{2}{5}$, $\frac{1}{3}$, and $\frac{4}{15}$.

Number	1	2	3	4	5
Multiples of 3	3	6	9	12	15
Multiples of 5	5	10	15		
Multiples of 15	15				

Fifteen is the smallest number that appears in each list. Therefore, the least common multiple of 5, 3, and 15 is 15. Change all the factors to have a denominator of 15.

$\frac{2}{5} = \frac{6}{15}, \frac{1}{3} = \frac{5}{15},$ and $\frac{4}{15}$ stays the same. So $\frac{4}{15} > \frac{5}{15} > \frac{6}{15}.$

So now that you know how to compare and order fractions, let's check back in with Shabang. Her previously ordered life is no longer in order.

Chapter 9
It All Adds Up

"Boys and girls. Line up, now," Mr. Little called as he exited the bus at the nursery with his foldable stool tucked under his arm. Today was the second field trip of Career Week, and he hoped it went better than the trip to the bank. *That* had been a disaster, first with robbers, and then poor Mayor Marbles who was still stuck in that vault.

Sticky jumped down from the top step of the bus and landed on his toes, ready. It wasn't that he was a bad kid, but trouble stuck to him like glue. Mr. Little sighed as he undid the stool and stepped up.

"You stay right by Ms. Shabang," he cautioned his troublesome student as the others began to emerge, "and don't touch a thing unless she says it's okay. Can you do that for me?"

Sticky nodded.

It was the best Mr. Little could hope for. He turned to the class. "Boys and girls! Here comes our guide."

"Good morning," the guide called, waving as he approached. "My name is Barry Bardely Barkensvelz, but call me Mr. Green." The name fit. He was dressed in green from the baseball cap on top of his head to his green Nikes.

He picked up a flowerpot full of rich, dark soil and held it so all could see. "We're going to have a great day, and we're going to start by talking about dirt. You can't grow beautiful plants without good food and vitamins."

"What's that?" Sticky asked, pointing to a shed behind Mr. Green.

"Great question, and just like it says, you must not go near there."

"Why, sir?" Egweena asked, wrinkling her forehead.

"Well, we use it for storage, and right now it is holding some very scary stuff that messes with the vitamins in the soil." Mr. Green ran his fingers through the dirt. "See, we use two different types of fertilizer to help the plants grow, but this time we got the wrong shipment. When we made our usual combination of $\frac{1}{2}$ of a teaspoon of the Plant Power and $\frac{1}{4}$ of the teaspoon of Booster Bang, the resulting $\frac{3}{4}$ of a teaspoon of fertilizer gave us quite a surprise. We got a lot more, and I do mean *a lot* more, plant growth than we bargained for. So we're sending it back."

Sticky's eyes were glued to the shed.

"Now class, look over here," Mr. Green said, directing their attention to a sampling of plants. "We have several plants that are alike and some that are different. Let's look at what they need to grow."

"Ms. Shabang?" Mr. Little prodded gently as the class began to meander after their guide. "You look a little peaked today. You feeling okay?"

Shabang nodded. "It's just my allergies."

Mr. Little smiled in sympathy. He'd never known Shabang to have allergies before, but there was always some new kind of pollutant in the air. "I need you to keep an especially careful eye on Sticky today."

"Good idea," Shabang agreed. "Let's put Sticky at the end of the line with me."

"Sticky?" Mr. Little called.

He was nowhere to be seen.

"It looks like the tour is going to have to wait," Mr. Green said. "Keep the children together. And keep an eye out for any unusual activity."

"Holy Moley! Unusual activity?" Mr. Little said, his voice quite a bit higher than usual. "Like what?"

It was then that they heard Sticky scream.

Oh, my!

While Mr. Little and Mr. Green go to see what trouble Sticky will be adding to this field trip, we can investigate a bit about how to add and subtract fractions.

You have known how to add and subtract for a long time—so long in fact that you don't think about what makes sense and what doesn't. You can subtract 20 students − 2 students = 18 students without thinking. But adding and subtracting fractions is different than adding and subtracting whole numbers, so let's take a closer look at the process.

When you add, you add units that are alike. It wouldn't make sense to say 2 frogs + 3 dragonflies = 5 frogs. That would be absurd adding.

And there is silly subtracting too. Say you have four piles with ten teddy bears in each, and you give away two bears, you wouldn't say 4 tens − 2 ones = 2.

The same is true with fractions. You can't add or subtract fractions unless they have the same units. And to have the same unit, they have to have—

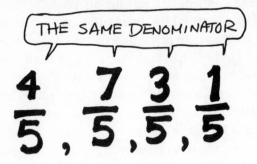

So first let's talk about these good fractions, the ones that work easily together. These fractions are ones that already, with no extra work on your part, have the same denominator. Any ideas how you might add $\frac{1}{2} + \frac{1}{2}$?

I'LL ADD 1+1 ON THE TOP FOR THE NUMERATOR: 1+1=2. THEN ADD 2+2 ON THE BOTTOM FOR THE DENOMINATOR: 2+2=4, THEN PUT THEM TOGETHER AND GET 2/4.

GOOD GRIEF. THAT DOESN'T MAKE SENSE. IT IS ADDING, BUT IF YOU HAD ½ OF A PEANUT BUTTER CREAM PIE + ANOTHER ½ OF A CHOCOLATE CREAM PIE, IS THAT EQUAL TO 2/4 OF A PIE?

Think about it.

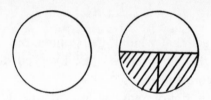

The fraction $\frac{2}{4}$ simplified using the GCF is the same as $\frac{1}{2}$, so you end up back where you started. So adding both the numerators and denominators doesn't work.

When adding or subtracting fractions, stop and consider what addition and subtraction mean.

So when you add, you are using a shortcut for counting and $\frac{2}{2}$ is another way of saying you have two parts of something divided into two. You have the whole thing, or one!

Let's try another one. Three kids each have a part of a giant funnel cake that was divided into four pieces. How much do they have together?

The problem in a math sentence would be written $\frac{1}{4} + \frac{1}{4} + \frac{1}{4} = $ _____ . Let's start by counting.

So the answer of $\frac{1}{4} + \frac{1}{4} + \frac{1}{4}$ is $\frac{3}{4}$.

Can you see that when the denominators are the same, you add up the numerators—just like you did when you counted on your fingers?

When the denominators are identical, subtraction works the same way. Say you cut an oxen leg into five pieces and a caveman has $\frac{4}{5}$ of it. His wife sneaks $\frac{1}{5}$ of the oxen leg away from him. How much does he have left?

Do you remember how you subtracted with your fingers? You simply counted backwards. Again when the denominators are the same, simply subtract the numerators. So what do you get?

$$\frac{4}{5} - \frac{1}{5} = \frac{3}{5}$$

Now you try a few pizza and breadstick fraction problems that hopefully won't leave you hungry:

1. $\frac{4}{5}$ of a pepperoni pizza + $\frac{2}{5}$ sausage pizza = how much meat pizza?

2. $\frac{2}{10}$ sardines pizza + $\frac{4}{10}$ jalapeno pizza = how much indigestion pizza?

3. Marshall has $\frac{6}{8}$ of a taco pizza. While he wasn't looking, his dog ate $\frac{3}{8}$ of the pizza. How much slobbered-on-pizza does he have left?

4. A baker's dozen of bread sticks (13) came with the pizza. Ahn ate $\frac{5}{13}$ of the breadsticks, Tomika ate $\frac{4}{13}$ of the breadsticks, and Juan ate the rest. What fraction of the breadsticks did Juan eat?

1. $\frac{4}{5} + \frac{2}{5} = \frac{6}{5}$ or $1\frac{1}{5}$ of meat pizzas.

2. $\frac{2}{10} + \frac{4}{10} = \frac{6}{10} = \frac{3}{5}$ of an indigestion pizza.

3. $\frac{6}{8} - \frac{3}{8} = \frac{3}{8}$ of a slobbered-on-pizza left.

4. One whole order of bread sticks − ($\frac{5}{13}$ Ahn ate + $\frac{4}{13}$ Tomika ate) = 1 − $\frac{6}{13}$ = $\frac{13}{13} - \frac{6}{13} = \frac{4}{13}$ of the breadsticks for Juan.

What do you do about those other fractions—the ones that don't have a common denominator?

If Egweena has $\frac{2}{3}$ of a brownie, and Sticky has $\frac{3}{10}$ of a brownie, do they have a whole brownie they can share?

You've probably never heard anyone count like this: "$\frac{1}{3}$, $\frac{2}{3}$, $\frac{3}{10}$, $\frac{4}{10}$, and $\frac{5}{10}$." The units don't count well together because they don't match. And if you add up the numerators of $\frac{2}{3} + \frac{3}{10}$ you get 2 + 3 = 5, but five *what?*

Good news! The LCM agent will be a great help with adding and subtracting fractions. Do you remember what he does?

That's right! The LCM can help with two fractions with different denominators like in the problem $\frac{2}{3} + \frac{3}{10}$. Here's a picture that may help you remember what he does.

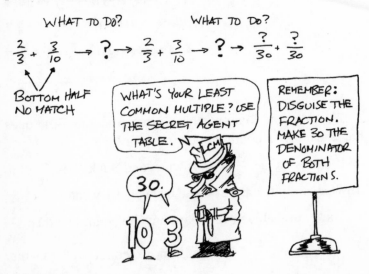

Remember the changed fractions have to be equivalent to the original fractions.

First, disguise $\frac{2}{3}$ so it has a denominator of thirty. What did you need to multiply three by to get thirty? That's right, 10.

Multiply the numerator by the same number that you multiplied the denominator.

$$\frac{2 \times 10}{3 \times 10} = \frac{20}{30}$$

So $\frac{2}{3} = \frac{20}{30}$.

Now disguise $\frac{3}{10}$ so it has a denominator of 30. What do you multiply 10 by to get 30? Correct: three.

So multiply the numerator by the same number you multiplied the denominator by.

$$\frac{3}{10} \times \frac{3}{3} = \frac{9}{30}$$

With the fractions disguised as $\frac{20}{30}$ and $\frac{9}{30}$, they are finally talking about the same units. You can add them. $\frac{20}{30} + \frac{9}{30} = \frac{29}{30}$, which is just $\frac{1}{30}$ shy of a whole Brownie.

See? That was easy!

Next, let's look at subtracting fractions with unlike denominators. Say you have a pumpkin pie that's divided into eight slices. You eat one piece, decide it's too hot, and place it in an open window to let it cool.

You still have $\frac{7}{8}$ of it left before the pie pirates happened by.

While no one is watching, the pirates start to take a whole piece and stop. One girl, though, decides a whole piece is too much, and, being the nice kid that she is, she makes a few cuts. Each of the pirates takes a smaller piece.

108

All together they take $\frac{4}{16}$ of the pie. How much do you have left?

IN CASE YOU WERE
CONFUSED BY ALL
THAT, THE MATH
SENTENCE IS

$$\frac{7}{8} - \frac{4}{16}$$

First, since the bottom halves don't match, find the LCM of the denominators. One of his tools is to use the secret agent table to find the multiples of both denominators:

Number	1	2
Multiples of 8	8	16
Multiples of 16	16	

Once you find the common multiple of sixteen, disguise both fractions to equivalent fractions that have that denominator.

STOP FOR
COMMON
MULTIPLES

First, disguise $\frac{7}{8}$ so it has a
denominator of sixteen. What did you
multiply eight by to get sixteen?

2

Multiply the numerator by the same number that you multiplied the denominator by.

$$\frac{7 \times 2}{8 \times 2} = \frac{14}{16}$$

So $\frac{7}{8} = \frac{14}{16}$.

The second fraction $\frac{4}{16}$ doesn't need a disguise because it has sixteen as its denominator. So the problem is $\frac{14}{16} - \frac{4}{16} = \frac{10}{16}$ piece of pumpkin pie.

Mmmm, $\frac{10}{16}$ is definitely not in its simplest form. This happens a lot when you add, subtract, multiply, and divide fractions. Can you make is simpler? (Remember Chapter 6.) Do you remember what the process was called?

Simplifying fractions.

110

What agent can help with this?

Now find the factors of both ten and sixteen. Then reduce $\frac{10}{16}$ for your final answer.

The factors of 10 are 1, 2, 5, 10.
The factors of 16 are 1, 2, 4, 8, 16.
So 2 is the GCF.
$$\frac{10 \div 2}{16 \div 2} = \frac{5}{8}$$
So the final, simplified answer is $\frac{5}{8}$.

But what if you have a whole or mixed number in the equation? What if you have two equal piles of gumballs with twelve gumballs in each pile, and your brother comes in and takes $1\frac{1}{3}$ pile? What fraction of a pile of gumballs do you have left?

One way to approach this is to think of two whole piles of gumballs as a fraction. A whole of anything is a fraction with a denominator of one. This is because the denominator tells the number of divisions, and the two piles of gumballs hadn't been divided. So two whole piles of gumballs are $\frac{2}{1}$.

The math problem is $\frac{2}{1} - 1\frac{1}{3}$.

First, change the second mixed number to an improper fraction.

$$\frac{2}{1} - \frac{4}{3}.$$

Next, find the LCM for the denominator.

Number	1	2	3
Multiples of 1	1	2	3
Multiple of 3			3

The LCM is 3.

Now change the first fraction to have a denominator of three.

$$\frac{2}{1} = \frac{6}{3}$$

Now subtract $\frac{6}{3} - \frac{4}{3}$. $\frac{2}{3}$ of a pile of gumballs are left.

If the problem was the addition problem of $2\frac{1}{3} + 3\frac{2}{3}$, you could add the whole numbers, and then add the fractions to get $5\frac{3}{3} = 6$.

With all these problems, the last step should always be to check your answer. You can Check It by adding or subtracting again, reversing the process, or using estimation.

You can check the above subtraction problem $2 - 1\frac{1}{3} = \frac{2}{3}$ by using addition: $\frac{2}{3} + 1\frac{1}{3} = 2$. You can check the previous addition problem $\frac{2}{3} + \frac{3}{10} = \frac{29}{30}$ by reversing the process and subtracting $\frac{29}{30} - \frac{3}{10} = \frac{29}{30} - \frac{9}{30} = \frac{20}{30} = \frac{2}{3}$.

Remember, to check subtraction problems, add, and to check addition problems, subtract.

Now here are a few problems created just for you by your very own fraction superhero, Silver. Make sure you check all your answers.

1. $\frac{4}{5} + \frac{3}{5}$

2. $\frac{8}{9} - \frac{4}{9}$

3. $\frac{2}{3} - \frac{1}{6}$

4. $\frac{6}{10} + \frac{3}{5}$

Of course, adding up fractions is one thing, but mixing together Plant Power and Booster Bang is another. Mr. Green was right. It sure was a lot more plant growth than they bargained for!

1. $\frac{4}{5} + \frac{3}{5} = \frac{7}{5} = 1\frac{2}{5}.$

2. $\frac{8}{9} - \frac{4}{9} = \frac{4}{9}.$

3. $\frac{2}{3} - \frac{1}{6} = $ ___. First give them the same denominators of six to get $\frac{4}{6} - \frac{1}{6} = \frac{3}{6}$ which is simplified as $\frac{1}{2}.$

4. $\frac{6}{10} + \frac{3}{5} = $ ___. First give them the same denominators of 10 to get $\frac{6}{10} + \frac{6}{10} = \frac{12}{10},$ which is simplified as $\frac{6}{5}$ and made into a mixed number of $1\frac{1}{5}.$

Chapter 10
Turbo Fractions

"I hear them," Dixie cried as she pulled frantically on the vines.

"Humph," Silver grunted not even taking the time to form a word. His hands flew faster than ever, chopping a large vine in half.

"Your turn," he said.

Dixie dropped to her knees and pulled hard. At first the stem resisted, tearing at her hand. Her arm hurt, her finger ached, but she held fast. Finally it yielded, flying into the air, roots and all. She threw it back over her shoulder to Mongrel, who grabbed it in his mouth and dragged it away.

"Okay," she said, taking in a deep breath. "$\frac{1}{2} + \frac{1}{2} + \frac{1}{2} + \frac{1}{2}$—"

"Turbo mode," Silver called.

Dixie reached out and grabbed a hunk of four vines, and yanked hard. "$\frac{1}{2} \times 4 = 2$. Much better," she said grabbing another chunk of vine.

And another. And another. Together they worked, Silver chopping, Dixie yanking, and Mongrel hauling the debris away. A small hole began to appear, tunneling through the mass of vines.

"Hang on!" Dixie yelled. "We're coming! Can anyone make it through?"

"I think so!" Mr. Little called back. "I'll send someone out."

Dixie and Silver stopped. Within a minute, a large boy appeared, crawling on his hands and knees, his face scratched and his shirt torn. But otherwise he was okay. "Send more," Silver called into the tunnel.

Soon Egweena, then others, emerged, one-by-one crawling into the light.

Finally, Mr. Little appeared.

"Okay?" Silver asked, giving the teacher a hand up.

Mr. Little nodded. "Yes, but the hole needs to be bigger for Mr. Green. He's bringing out Sticky."

"And Ms. Shabang?" Dixie asked.

Mr. Little looked around. "I thought she was with you." Together they turned, making a full circle, looking, wondering, but Shabang wasn't there.

Vines, and bruises, and missing people! The good news was all the students were safe. The bad news was, some seemed scratched up a bit.

In this chapter, there is also good news and bad news. First, multiplying fractions is easier than adding and subtracting, because there are no disguises. You don't have to find the LCM.

THAT'S NOT GOOD NEWS FOR ME.

But this chapter only dips its big toe into the world of multiplying. It only looks at multiplying fractions by whole numbers.

And before we learn how to multiply fractions, we need to look at what multiplication is.

Basically, multiplication adds turbo speed to addition.

That's the purpose of multiplication—to speed things up. The problem 5×6 says add the number 6 to itself five times: $6 + 6 + 6 + 6 + 6 = 30$.

The second way to think of multiplication is in terms of groups. The problem of 5×6 can be thought of as five groups of howling dog singers with six in each group.

So multiplication can be thought of as either *turbo addition* or the *great grouper*.

Notice, when you multiply two whole numbers greater than one, your answer is always bigger than both the numbers you started with. So $5 \times 6 = 30$.

Take the problem $6 \times \dfrac{1}{2} =$ _____. Knowing that multiplication is turbo addition, can you find the answer?

Use your excellent fraction addition skills to add $\dfrac{1}{2}$ to itself six different times: $\dfrac{1}{2} + \dfrac{1}{2} + \dfrac{1}{2} + \dfrac{1}{2} + \dfrac{1}{2} + \dfrac{1}{2}$.

Or you can use the great grouper approach. Think of $6 \times \frac{1}{2}$ as $\frac{1}{2}$ of a group with six dogs.

This group approach brings up an important point about multiplying fractions. Think of $6 \times \frac{1}{2}$ as $\frac{1}{2}$ of 6. When you are multiplying fractions and having a hard time understanding what it means, replace the multiplication symbol with the word *of*.

So imagine $\frac{1}{2}$ of the 6 dogs.

While it is a multiplication problem, it seems like division. When you multiply by a proper fraction, your answer does end up smaller. This is because to get the answer you divide the group of six in half. So what is $\frac{1}{2}$ of 6?

The answer is three, so you see how using either the addition or the great grouper way can solve the problem. But, since multiplication is turbo addition, surely there is a quicker turbo way.

When you multiply whole numbers you use your memorized multiplication tables. So, when you multiply fractions, you do the same.

No stop! You don't need to learn multiplication tables for all the fractions. You use the multiplication tables you already know.

I DON'T NEED ANY MORE STRESS.

Great news!

You simply multiply the numerators by each other and the denominators by each other. The product of the two numerators becomes the new numerator. The product of the two denominators becomes the new denominator. Easy! Right?

$$\frac{\text{NUMERATOR} \times \text{NUMERATOR}}{\text{DENOMINATOR} \times \text{DENOMINATOR}} = \frac{\text{NEW NUMERATOR}}{\text{NEW DENOMINATOR}}$$

Now let's do $6 \times \dfrac{1}{2}$ and prove that it works.

SOMETHING IS MISSING.

Yikes! Six doesn't have a denominator. Can you give six a denominator without changing its value? Remember the answer is simply one. Six is equal to $\dfrac{6}{1}$. It means six candy bars are divided into one piece, which is exactly the same as six whole candy bars.

$$\frac{6 \times 1}{1 \times 2} = \frac{6}{2}$$

Finally, make $\frac{6}{2}$ a mixed number.

$$\frac{6}{2} = 3$$

How about another problem?

Mr. Little has told Mr. Green that $\frac{1}{4}$ of the kids in his fifth grade class have flunked the science test on plants. He has twenty kids in his class. Mr. Green wants to figure out how many flunked. First he finds the fraction equation, and then he solves the problem.

$$20 \times \frac{1}{4}$$

$$\frac{20}{1} \times \frac{1}{4} = \frac{20}{4}$$

$$\frac{20}{4} = \frac{10}{2} = 5 \text{ kids flunked.}$$

With all these multiplication problems an important last step is to check your answer.

With multiplication you can Check It by redoing the multiplication problem, dividing it, or estimating. Often the best way to Check It is to divide.

CHECK IT ✓

So if $20 \times \dfrac{1}{4} = 5$, then to Check It do $5 \div 20$, and you should get $\dfrac{1}{4}$ or try $5 \div \dfrac{1}{4}$ and you should get 20. This dividing of fractions is the subject of our next chapter.

But before you move on, here are a couple more dips into the pool of fraction multiplication:

1. $\dfrac{1}{4} \times 6 =$

2. $\dfrac{1}{5} \times 10 =$

3. $9 \times \dfrac{1}{2} =$

1. $\dfrac{6}{4} = \dfrac{3}{2} = 1\dfrac{1}{2}$; 2. $\dfrac{10}{5} = 2$; 3. $\dfrac{9}{2} = 4\dfrac{1}{2}$

Fabulous! There is more to learn but you've gotten a great start. Let's check in with Silver, who is still in turbo speed, before sticking our little toe into the division pool.

"Do you think it is wide enough?" Dixie asked, eying the tunnel as she flipped a vine over her head.

Mongrel paused, took a hard look at the opening, and yelped once.

"I agree," Dixie said. "Silver, stop. Mr. Green can get through."

Instantly Silver ceased, and a rustle of movement swelled toward them. First a foot, then a leg with a wrinkled sock, followed by a simple one-piece dress, and finally a whole, slim body.

"Shabang!" Mr. Little called. He came over and gave his assistant a huge hug. "We thought you were lost."

"Not to worry," Shabang said, mostly embarrassed by the embrace. "I was helping with Sticky. He broke his arm, you know."

"But I didn't see you—"

"Can you give me a hand?" a voice interrupted.

Chapter 11
The Flip Side

"Ms. Shabang!" Mr. Little said, dusting himself off as he got up. "Who's with the class? Is everything okay?"

"Everything is fine," Shabang answered. "I asked Dixie to step in for a minute. "I have cafeteria duty, you know."

Mr. Little studied her for a moment. "You seem different," he said. He couldn't quite put his finger on what it was, but Shabang was usually so quiet and settled, not bustling about like today.

"Oh, just in a hurry," she said, rushing off. "Can't be late!"

Mr. Little frowned. He didn't have much time to think about it. He was too worried about Sticky. The whole time he was in the principal's office, Sticky insisted that he hadn't spread the fertilizer, and Mr. Little was inclined to believe him.

After all, Sticky liked bragging about trouble he'd attracted, but not this time. Over and over he said he hadn't done it, but if not, who else could it have been, and why?

Shabang bounced on toward the cafeteria. Yesterday had been a close call. Too close. She'd stepped away for a minute to bury the keys, and that silly Sticky almost caught her!

What if they'd seen her? Then she'd have ended up in jail, right along with, well, you know, the *other* Shabang, the *old* one.

It was really unnerving having two personalities. Old Shabang could pop in at any moment, and Old Shabang was

B-O-R-I-N-G! She couldn't deal with anything being chopped up, divided, or broken into parts, which was why she took the keys! To her, they were a whole, and she didn't want them to be given to three different people like they were each just a third of something.

Truth was New Shabang, or Newsie as she liked to call herself, was having a great time. Newsie smiled as she wound through the students entering the cafeteria. She spied Sticky at the back of the line. She was supposed to make sure the kids didn't cut, but maybe today she'd flip things and let the back of the line go first. She felt bad he was getting blamed for the fertilizer episode, but it couldn't be helped. She couldn't tell, unless she gave up the keys, and then what?

The mayor was okay. She'd heard he'd lost a little weight, but he could use a bit of reduction. The superheroes would think of something.

Meanwhile she had to get the children lined up to eat.

"I've got a fun surprise for all of you," she said to the children.

And while Newsie flips the lunch line around to let Sticky go first, let's talk about division of fractions which also deals with flipping.

Fractions are, in fact, a special form of division. When you use the fraction $\frac{1}{2}$ you are actually talking about division. After all, $\frac{1}{2}$ is the same as one divided by two, and $\frac{1}{3}$ is the same as one divided by three. (You will learn more about this in Chapter 16.)

But this chapter is not about what makes up a fraction, it's about division problems that contain a fraction. This chapter only dips its little toe into the division fraction pool.

It only talks about division problems where a whole number is divided by a fraction.

First, let's look at what division is. Division is the inverse of multiplication. It's the flip side.

Think about the problem $15 \div 5$. It means subtract five from fifteen until you end up with zero.

The second way to think of division is in terms of groups. Remember the howling dogs from the last chapter? If your problem is $30 \div 6$, think of it as how many groups of six are there in thirty howling dogs.

So division can be thought of as *turbo subtraction* and the *great dividing grouper*.

With whole numbers, if you have twenty-four cookies and six friends who want to share, division will help you determine how many to give each friend: $24 \div 6 = 4$.

When you work with fractions, it's the same. Say you have six licorice ropes. Instead of dividing them by a whole number, you divide them by the fraction $\frac{1}{2}$. You are asking the question: How many halves are there in six?

To find the answer you could use a picture.

Note that each group is $\frac{1}{2}$ of a piece of licorice rope, so you are figuring out how many times $\frac{1}{2}$ goes into 6.

Or you use subtraction and subtract $\frac{1}{2}$ from 6 until you get 0.

Yes! Since multiplication is turbo addition, division can be thought of as turbo subtraction. Remember the turbo scooter?

You can change a division problem to multiplication and solve it by flipping.

You do flip, but you don't put the whole equation upside down. Instead you flip the second number over, which in this case is the fraction, and then flip the division symbol to make it multiplication.

Take a look.

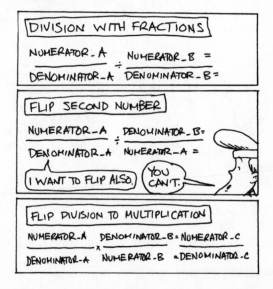

In a nutshell here's how you divide by a fraction.

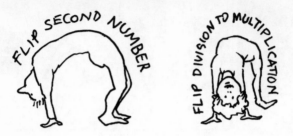

Here's a demo from Mini and Max who come to us from the beginning of the book.

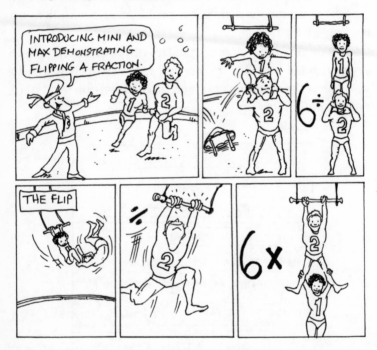

So with a little trapeze work, the equation $6 \div \frac{1}{2}$ becomes $6 \times \frac{2}{1}$, and that's easy to solve.

Do you remember how to make six into a fraction? Right, it's $\frac{6}{1}$. So our new equation is $\frac{6}{1} \times \frac{2}{1} = \frac{12}{1} = 12$.

Even if it doesn't seem right, it is. The reason is because multiplication and division are the flip side of each other.

In fact there's a famous saying about division and fractions.

PAUSE FOR MIXED THOUGHT

Let's say for your birthday party you have twelve pizzas and every person invited can eat $\frac{1}{4}$ of a pizza. How many people can you invite? What is the problem?

The problem is $12 \div \frac{1}{4}$.

Now solve it!

$$\frac{12}{1} \div \frac{1}{4}$$

With a good flip it becomes

$$\frac{12}{1} \times \frac{4}{1} = \frac{48}{1}$$

And $\frac{48}{1}$ = 48 people.

Finally, with all division problems, an important last step is to check your answer.

With division, you can Check 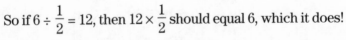 It by redoing the division problem, multiplying or estimating. Often the best way to Check It is to multiply.

So if $6 \div \frac{1}{2} = 12$, then $12 \times \frac{1}{2}$ should equal 6, which it does!

Also, if $12 \div \frac{1}{4} = 48$, then $48 \times \frac{1}{4}$ should and does equal 12.

Now you try. You can either subtract, using the great division grouper approach, or flip and multiply. Remember

132

in Chapter 10 you learned that you should check your fraction multiplication answers by dividing. These problems will help check some of the answers in Chapter 10.

1. $3 \div \dfrac{1}{2}$

2. $5 \div \dfrac{1}{4}$

1. This is to check the problem $6 \times \dfrac{1}{2}$ in Chapter 10. $3 \div \dfrac{1}{2} = 3 \times \dfrac{2}{1} = \dfrac{6}{1} = 6$.

2. This is to check the problem in Chapter 10 about how many kids in Mr. Little's class flunked: $20 \times \dfrac{1}{4} = 5$. $5 \div \dfrac{1}{4} = 5 \times \dfrac{4}{1} = \dfrac{20}{1} = 20$. If you used the grouper or subtraction approach, you can figure out how many times the fraction goes into one and then multiply that answer by the whole number (for example, $5 \div \dfrac{1}{4}$). You can figure that $\dfrac{1}{4}$ goes into one 4 times, so it would go into five $5 \times 4 = 20$ times.

Great! Now let's see how Shabang is doing in the cafeteria.

"How's your arm, Sticky?" Newsie asked as she slipped in beside Sticky. Her lunch duty was over, so she had a little time to relax.

"Fine, ma'am," Sticky said with a grin. "Would you like to sign my cast?"

What fun, Newsie thought. She'd never signed a cast before, but then she'd never known anyone who'd broken an arm before, either. She pulled out a pen from her pocket, drew three small cut flowers tied by a bow, and printed her name.

She smiled. Old Shabang hated cut flowers. Drawing three separate blooms would have driven her crazy. But not Newsie! Fractions? No problem. Cutting? Chopping? What fun!

And for now that was all that mattered.

Chapter 12
Parting Is Such Sweet Sorrow

While our superheroes make their way to the scene, we can use this time to figure out what the decimal one and six-tenths really means.

This decimal language isn't new, though, because when you know something about fractions, you know something about decimals. Why? Because decimals and fractions have a lot in common.

Dixie and Silver are both correct, and hungry. Decimals and fractions are two different ways to say the same thing.

But decimals look totally different than fractions. Fractions have numerators and denominators, but decimals have digits in two different zones.

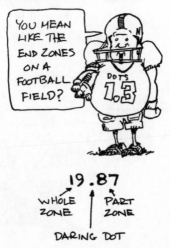

19.87

WHOLE ZONE

PART ZONE

DARING DOT

135

The Whole Zone is a place for the whole number, and the Part Zone is a place for the decimal part. The Daring Dot is the alias of the decimal point. It separates the Whole Zone from the Part Zone.

Everything in the Part Zone is between the zero and one. Numbers like 0.3 or 0.78 or 0.764567 or even 0.87234 are all between zero and one.

But what if the number has digits in both the Whole and Part Zones; where does it go on the number line? It's not between zero and one, but it is between two whole numbers.

Think about it. How many hot dogs are 4.8?

On the number line 4.8 hot dogs is between four and five.

4.8 HOT DOGS

A number with a decimal is between the value of its whole number and the next whole number, so you know generally that 4.8 is between four and five. But surely 4.8 means something more specific.

I SEE YOU NEED A QUICK REVIEW ABOUT PLACE VALUE

TO KNOW WHAT A NUMBER MEANS WE LOOK TO THE PLACES VALUE OF ITS DIGITS. TAKE THE NUMBER 4,356. IT MEANS...

4   3   5 6
4 THOUSANDS 3 HUNDREDS 5 10s 6 1s

Do you see that each place has a meaning and the places relate to each other? What happens when you move from the four to the three or from the three to the five?

That's correct. When you move one place to the right, the place value has one less zero. To get one less zero, you divide each place value by ten.

Start with 1,000	thousands
1,000 ÷ 10 = 100	hundreds
100 ÷ 10 = 10	tens
10 ÷ 10 = 1	ones
Daring Dot	.

Don't stop!

$$1 \div 10 = \frac{1}{10} \qquad \text{tenths}$$

$$\frac{1}{10} \div 10 = \frac{1}{100} \qquad \text{hundredths}$$

$$\frac{1}{100} \div 10 = \frac{1}{1000} \qquad \text{thousandths}$$

YES, YOU COULD KEEP GOING AND I COULD KEEP SHOOTING AND MAKING SMALLER DECIMALS.

And here is another illustration of place values laid out from left to right.

THOUSANDS   HUNDREDS TENS ONES • TENTHS HUNDREDTHS THOUSANDTHS

When you see what place the digits occupy, you know the value of the decimal. The number 2357.234 is two thousand three hundred fifty-seven and two hundred thirty-four thousandths.

So the number 4.8 means four whole hot dogs, and since the eight is in the tenths place, eight tenths of the next one.

The number 2.34 means you read two whole books, and since the four is in the hundredths place, thirty-four hundredths of the next.

But how do you know the names of all the places to the right of the decimal?

Do you see that the whole numbers have "th" twins in the Part Zone? On the whole number side, you have tens. On the part number side you have tenths. So for every place in the Whole Zone, with one exception, there is a place in the Part Zone that ends with "th."

Tens means how many groups of 10s. Tenths means the whole has been divided into ten parts.

The values of the numbers in the Part Zone are a fraction of the value of the number in the Whole Zone. Again there is one exception. Does anyone see it? One does not have a part twin.

And the ones place is the only place that doesn't have a part twin.

While it would make it easier to remember if there was an oneth place, it wouldn't make sense. A oneth isn't a part. It would be just $\frac{1}{1}$, and $\frac{1}{1}$ is one, so our ones place will have to be without a part twin.

Let's look at a picture that shows what decimals mean.

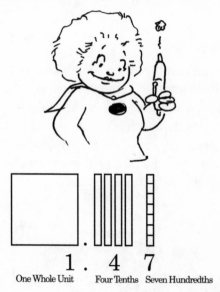

1 . 4 7

One Whole Unit   Four Tenths Seven Hundredths

The ones place represents a whole one, in this case one whole box.

The tenths place is the whole box divided into ten equal strips. Since there is a four in the tenths place, the tens place shows four of those strips.

The hundredth place would be the whole box divided into a hundred equal pieces, and since there is a seven in that place, there are only seven hundredths.

PAUSE FOR
DARING
THOUGHT

What are the positions of the underlined numbers?

1. 34.56<u>7</u>
2. <u>9</u>856.21
3. <u>4</u>5.45
4. 45.<u>4</u>5

1. 7 is in the thousandths place; 2. 9 is in the thousands place; 3. 4 is in the tens place; 4. 4 is in the tenths place.

Notice again that the names of position of the seven and the nine are remarkably similar. They are thousands and thousandths. The thousandths is the "th" twin in the Part Zone. Also, the tens and the tenths sound a lot alike. The tenths is the tens "th" twin in the Part Zone.

This brings us to the proper way to say decimals. First, look at the official way to say decimals.

THE OFFICIAL
WAY TO SAY
DECIMALS:
READ THE
WHOLE ZONE
NUMBER IF
THERE IS ONE.

1. Read the Whole Zone number if there is one.

2. If there is a whole number, the word *and* is said when reading the Daring Dot. It is the only place *and* is said. If there isn't a whole number part, don't say *and*.

3. Read the number in the Part Zone like you would read a whole number. End with the place value of the right most digit. (Remember that it should have the "th" sound.)

4. Money is a decimal also, but it is said in a different way. For more on this see Chapter 12.5.

Time for some practice. How would you read 1.5? Right. You would say one and five tenths. How about 523.34? Be careful with the *and*.

When you say numbers, if the *and* is going to mean anything, you can't throw it in any old place.

THAT'S THE OFFICIAL WAY, BUT US PEOPLE ON THE STREET SAY IT DIFFERENT. WE USE "POINT" INSTEAD OF AN "AND" IT'S MORE STYLISH. WE WOULD SAY 523.34 LIKE FIVE HUNDRED TWENTY-THREE POINT THIRTY FOUR.

STOP YOUR WICKED WAYS. IT ISN'T THE RIGHT WAY TO SAY DECIMALS.

Now see if you can say decimals correctly. Remember, the Mathopolis police officer is watching.

1. 0.412
2. 4.05
3. 456.1
4. Extra bonus points 345.6578

1. four hundred twelve thousandths;
2. four and five hundredths;
3. four hundred fifty-six and one tenth;
4. three hundred forty-five thousand five hundred seventy-eight ten-thousandths.

Now you know the place value of decimals, how to figure out the names of the decimals, and the rules for saying them, but you don't know whether or not our superheroes have arrived back at the bank.

143

"Thank goodness you're here!" Trusty Dusty called as the superheroes rushed in. "It's the mayor. His air supply is messed up, and he only has a few more minutes."

Dixie pushed the intercom button and put a smile in her voice. "Hey there, Mayor Marbles. How's your little vacation going?"

"It'd be going better," the mayor replied, "if I had one of your sweet potato pies."

"I tell you what I'll do," Dixie went on. "When you get out, I'll cook everything you want."

"Now that sounds like something worth waiting for," Mayor Marbles said. "Any idea—how—much—"

"The compressors are here," a workman called in the door. "I got three. I didn't know which one was one and six tenths."

"Just in time!" Silver said running for the door. "The mayor is fading!"

"Let's see if Mayor Marbles is okay!" Dixie said.

Silver nodded, and the two raced downstairs where Trusty met them with a wide grin.

"The mayor says he's just had the best nap," Trusty said. "Probably low oxygen."

"Nick of time!" Silver said.

Yes," Dixie declared. "That was too close!"

They looked at each other, and as if they'd rehearsed, shouted together with renewed determination, "KEYS!"

Chapter 12.5
Right on the Money

She called me "Lawrence," Mr. Little thought as he gathered up his stool. He knew people changed, but Shabang's new attitude was disturbing.

"Mr. Little?" Sticky called as the bus lurched forward. "Do you think they'll give us some marbles?"

"Oh, I don't think—"

"How far is it, sir?" interrupted Egweena.

"About ten miles," Mr. Little answered.

"Ten more miles to the factory," sang Sticky in a voice you would expect from someone with his name. "Ten more miles to go. Ten more mile, ten more miles, ten more miles—"

"Sticky, please stop that repeating song," Mr. Little said.

"Nine more miles to the factory," sang Sticky.

Mr. Little started down the aisle. He'd barely taken two steps when Shabang brushed by.

"I got this, Shrimp," Shabang said without breaking stride. "Or maybe I should say three tenths of a shrimp."

Shrimp? Did Shabang just call Mr. Little *Shrimp*?

Well! Wars have been fought over insults like this, but more wars have been fought over one very special decimal.

PAUSE FOR IMPORTANT THOUGHT

Can you guess what it is?

The answer is money, money, and more money.

Whether you have $3.99, $56.88, or $1,234.87, you have money and, at the same time, a decimal, even though you say money differently. People don't say $4.55 as four dollars and fifty-five hundredth, although that is technically what it means. They say four dollars and fifty-five cents.

The decimal part is read as *cents*. Why? The word *cents* actually is from an old French word meaning hundred and the Latin word *centum*, so when you talk about cents you are talking about hundredth of a dollar.

So how do dollars related to decimals?

A dollar is a whole. It is one, and to get part of the dollar you use coins.

As Dixie said, a quarter is 0.25, which is twenty-five hundredths. It can also be written $\frac{25}{100}$. You probably think of a quarter as $\frac{1}{4}$ of a dollar, which is what $\frac{25}{100}$ is after it has been reduced.

A dime is 0.1 or one-tenth of a dollar, which can also be written $\frac{1}{10}$. A nickel is 0.05 or five hundredths of a dollar, which can also be written $\frac{5}{100}$ of a dollar. You probably think of a nickel as $\frac{1}{20}$ of a dollar. And that is exactly what $\frac{5}{100}$ is after it's been reduced. A penny is 0.01 or one hundredth of a dollar, which can also be written $\frac{1}{100}$.

Notice that the dollar is in the ones position because the dollar is one whole. The dime is the tenths position. The penny is the hundredths position.

Often when you have a number with two digits after the decimal point, thinking of it in terms of money can be helpful. If you think of 1.04 in terms of dollars, dimes, and pennies, what is it?

One dollar and 0.04 is four pennies. A penny is $\frac{1}{100}$ of a dollar, so 0.04 is $\frac{4}{100}$.

Now try 3.57, with only dollars, dimes, and pennies.

It has 3 dollars, 5 dimes (or $\frac{5}{10}$), and 7 pennies (or $\frac{7}{100}$).

Great job, now let's move on and talk about a couple other kinds of decimals besides money.

So far all the decimals you've seen, whether money or not, have been a kind of decimal called *terminating* decimals. What does terminating mean?

Terminate means *to end*, so terminating decimals are decimals that end, or stop, like 2.3 and 4.569837. So what's the opposite of decimals that end?

Of course! Decimals that don't end! They go on and on and on, like some people, who shall remain nameless, do when they are singing on the bus.

Those decimals that go on and on are called *infinite* decimals or *nonterminating* decimals. When you learn how to change fractions to decimals, you will learn that some common fractions are very difficult and don't make terminating fractions.

There are two kinds of these nonterminating decimals: one kind is *repeating*, and the other is *nonrepeating*.

149

Repeating decimals are just like repeating silly jokes. One or more digits repeat in a pattern like the mayor's "Pete and Repeat." With the decimal 0.33333333333333333333333333 etc., threes go on repeating infinitely which make it a repeating nonterminating decimal, written like $0.\overline{33}$.

The line on top of the threes symbolizes that the threes go on and on. These are decimals that have a pattern to their repeating numbers.

There are also numbers that are nonterminating and *nonrepeating*. One of the most famous is the decimal equivalent for *pi*, a term that represents a number mathematicians use a lot. Simply put, pi is a nonterminating, nonrepeating decimal value that is used for calculating the area and circumference of a circle. It is written as ≠ and means 3.141592+ with the plus meaning the decimals go on and on and on with no repeating pattern.

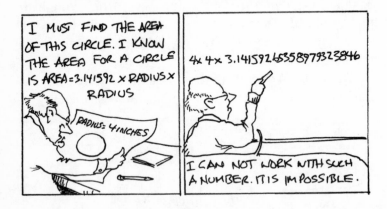

All these nonterminating numbers bring up a good point, and that point is rounding.

What if you have the number 1.$\overline{33}$, and you need to add it to the number 2.34? What do you do?

You round, which means you get rid of some of the digits, so the numbers are easier to work with or write. Even if you wanted to write pi all the way out, you couldn't since it's infinite. You have to round.

When you round whole numbers, you turn some digits to zero, like 356 rounded to the nearest 100 becomes 400. When you round decimals, you don't need to add zeroes; instead, you get rid of the digits. Here are the steps:

1. *Keep or Throw.* To round you first decide how many digits to keep. This depends on how specific you need to be. If you are working with money, and the number $5.7645, you only need to keep two places after the decimal.

2. *Underline.* Underline the last digit you are going to keep: $5.7<u>6</u>45

   UNDER

3. *Tug-of-War.* Look closely at the digit to the right of the underlined digit 6. How strong is that four? Is it strong enough to pull the six up to a seven or does the six remain a six? The superhero secret to make this decision is to remember that a number must be five or greater to pull the underlined number up, and it must be four or less to keep the unlined number the same. The four is weak, so the digit stays as a six.

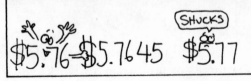

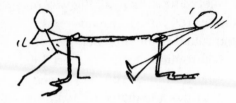

4. *Wipe 'Em Out.* Wipe out all the other digits to the right of the underlined number.

Remember the steps: Keep or Throw, Underline, Tug-of-War, and Wipe 'Em Out.

Now, you give it a try.

1. Take the repeating decimal for $\frac{1}{3}$ which is $0.\overline{33}$, and round it to the nearest thousandth place.
2. Take the nonrepeating decimal of pi 3.14159265358979323846 and round it to the nearest ten-thousandths.

1. 0.333; 2. 3.1416

One more thing before you move on. Here are a few quick words about decimal and the zero.

Yes, zero is nothing but it has a very important function. It is a place holder. Take a look at these numbers and you'll understand how important zero can be.

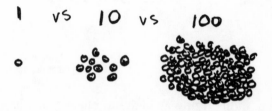

The only digit added is zero, but the numbers are completely different.

With decimals, zeroes are also place holders. But with decimals you hold the place in a different position.

$$.1 = .10 = .100 = .10000$$

Those zeroes aren't holding a place. Here come some zeroes who know how to do their job.

$$0.1 \neq 0.01 \neq 0.001 \neq 0.0001$$

In the Part Zone, if you put zeroes before the digits it makes the numbers different because the digit with a value is in a different place. Also, if you only have zeroes it doesn't matter how many you have, they are all the same numbers.

$$0 = 0.0 = 00.0 = 0.00$$

Now that you know something about zeroes holding place value, do you know which number is more: 0.05 or 0.5 or 0.50?

0.5 and 0.50 are the same and they are more than 0.05.

If you didn't know which number was more, don't worry; that's the topic of our next chapter. But first, let's check and see how Mr. Little feels about Shabang calling him *Shrimp*.

"Ms. Shabang," Mr. Little said as they disembarked from the bus. "May I have a word?"

"Sure thing, Shorts," Shabang said. "But Egweena said she needs to do her business before we start on our tour. Wouldn't want her to do it in her pants while we chat, would you?"

"Awk 'b-sha-ra-ra." Mr. Little fought to make some intelligent sound. Finally he found his tongue.

"MS. SHABANG! You've gone too far!" he shouted, but the words fell apart in the air. Shabang was out of hearing distance.

Chapter 13

Line 'Em Up

Newsie chuckled to herself as she stood outside the girl's restroom waiting for Egweena. Mr. Little had bristled worse than a porcupine when she'd called him Shrimp, but, after all, he was shorter then most of the kids. If the shoe fit, he needs to wear it and all that.

She remembered once when they were studying the meter he'd attached a measuring tape to the wall and had all the kids line up. Then he'd measure everyone—except himself.

They'd made a table and compared their heights.

NAME	HEIGHT/METERS
BIG KID	1·62 METERS
EGWEENA	1·52 METERS
STICKY	1·42 METERS

Newsie smiled at the thought. Mr. Little had gotten down off his stool only once the whole lesson because he knew some of the kids were taller. It was then that Newsie had seen how tall he was, 1.47. If she knew anything about comparing decimals, she knew that would put him between Egweena and Sticky in the height table. So he had no right to be mad at her for speaking the truth.

Still, if he was going to chew someone out, Newsie figured it might as well be Old Shabang. The old girl would be surprised to find herself standing in the middle of Mathopolis's Marble Factory, but hey, she could handle it. She was tough.

Newsie smoothed her hair back into a sleek, tight bun, straightened the top of her boots and took a deep breath. Then with a sigh she let go, and Old Shabang popped out.

Poor Shabang! Imagine what it would feel like to suddenly be in the middle of a marble factory with no idea how you got there.

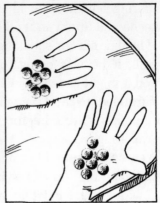

Chances are, even Shabang who is very confused can compare these two decimals and come up with the correct answer without even engaging her brain. Chances are you also know Sticky's left hand has more money. You can figure it out because you know how to compare whole numbers, and most of what you know about comparing whole numbers applies to decimals.

But when you compare decimals, you need to be careful. They can be tricky.

So let's take a closer look. Who has more money, the mayor locked in the vault or Silver in his pocket?

It probably didn't even take you a second to answer the question. It's because the $3,456,745.00 has a lot more digits than $3.25. You could tell $3,456,745.00 was more just by looking at it.

With whole positive numbers, more digits make bigger numbers because as digits move to the left, numbers get larger. But this isn't true of decimals because when decimals get more digits, they are added to the right. And remember, positions to the right have increasingly smaller values. So with decimals, longer numbers aren't necessarily bigger. The number 0.456453453 is less than 0.5, even though it has a lot more digits.

MORE DIGITS ≠ LARGER NUMBER

So when you are comparing, it's no longer about what is the longest number. A good place to start comparing is to begin to call numbers by their proper names.

If you have the numbers 0.45 and 0.56 and say forty-five hundredths and fifty-six hundredths, you know fifty-six is greater.

But sometimes calling a number by its proper name doesn't help with decimals, especially if they have different place values like 0.5 and 0.51. With these numbers you are comparing five-tenths and fifty-one hundredths.

In cases like this, look at the place of the digits and only compare the value of the digits that occupy the same place.

So how do you make sure you are comparing digits with the same place value? Well, you do what a cowboy does and "Line 'Em Up."

Line 'Em Up by their place value. A quick way to do this is to line up the decimal points. Then all the place values will line up and be easy to compare.

There always has to be someone in the crowd. If you're penmanship-challenged like the medieval man, you can use a table to compare 0.5 and 0.51. First, write all the digits in the appropriate columns.

	Ones	Daring Dot	Tenths	Hundredths
0.5	0	.	5	
0.51	0	.	5	1

After you have them lined up, move from left to right and compare the digits in each column with each other.

Compare them. You have a blank, which is like a 0, versus a 1. Is one digit greater than the other? Do you have a winner?

Yes. After going from left to right, column by column, 0.51 finally has a digit greater than 0.5; therefore, 0.51 is greater than 0.5: 0.51 > 0.5.

So here, in a nutshell, are the steps you need to know to compare decimal numbers.

1. LINE 'EM UP ••••••• ON THE DARING DOT. IF ONE NUMBER HAS A LARGER PLACE VALUE THAN THE OTHERS, IT IS THE GREATER NUMBER. IF YOU ARE ONLY COMPARING TWO NUMBERS, YOU ARE DONE.

2. COMPARE. IF THE FIRST DIGITS HAVE THE SAME PLACE VALUE, COMPARE THEM. IF THEY ARE DIFFERENT YOU ARE DONE. IF YOU KEEP COMPARING AND ONE NUMBER RUNS OUT OF DIGITS, THE OTHER NUMBER IS GREATER.

MY CLUB IS BIGGER THAN YOURS. THIS IS THE SYMBOL FOR "COMPARE"

Oops! We forgot to mention one thing: a prestep, something you have to do before you begin. You have to Inspect the Units.

If you are comparing numbers that have a unit, like meters or ounces or feet, both numbers must be talking about the same unit. You can't compare one number that refers to centimeters with another that represents meters. One number in inches cannot be compared to a number in feet until they have been converted to the same units.

Let's try a problem of who weighs the most. Sticky has a dog that weighs 23.6 pounds. Egweena is always bragging that her cat, who weighs 376.96 ounces, is bigger. So who's right?

Unit Inspection

Uh, oh. They are not the same. Egweena is talking ounces, and Sticky is talking pounds. So change 376.96 ounces to pounds by dividing by 16 (because there are sixteen ounces in a pound). 376.96 ÷ 16 = 23.56 pounds. Now you can compare.

Line 'Em Up   LINE 'EM UP ●●●●●●●●

Both numbers have a digit in the tens place value, so you need to compare the first digits. They are the same, so move right. Compare each set of digits until you get one that is greater?

Compare

Now you try. Which number is larger, 83.875 or 83.78? Line 'Em Up and Compare.

83.875 is larger than 83.78.

Tens	Ones	Daring Dot	Tenths	Hundredths	Thousandths
Same	Same				
8	3	.	8	7	5
8	3	.	7	8	
			Top is larger so stop		

Remember, comparing decimals isn't about which number has the most digits that are greater. It's about which number has the most *significant* digit that is the greatest. The tenths place is more significant than the hundredths, and the hundredths place is more significant than the thousandths. A bigger place value makes a digit more significant.

But what if you have more than two numbers and need to put them in order? Well, ordering is like comparing only with more numbers. Say you had to order the following numbers: 45.3, 45, 234.898, and 0.301.

You know numbers often come without decimal points. So if they don't have a decimal point, because they are whole numbers, put one where it belongs.

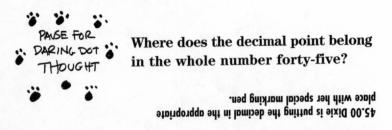

Where does the decimal point belong in the whole number forty-five?

45.00 Dixie is putting the decimal in the appropriate place with her special marking pen.

Yes! The decimal point comes after the whole number because it separates the Whole Zone from the Part Zone. So now line up the decimal points and compare.

Hundreds	Tens	Ones	Daring Dot	Tenths	Hundredths	Thousandths
	4	5	.	3		
	4	5	.	0		
2	3	4	.	8	9	8
		0	.	3	0	1

Remember, start with the leftmost digit. The two is all by itself in the hundreds column. Since no other number has a value in the hundredths column, you know that 234.898 is the biggest number. But what about the rest of the numbers?

That's a good question. If you are ordering all the numbers, you can't stop when you find the biggest. Putting the number 234.898 aside, you must continue to compare the other numbers. Like Dixie says, bring on the digits from the next column: the tens column.

Compare them: A four is in the tens position in both the numbers 45.3 and 45, so it's a tie. (The other number, 0.301, doesn't have anything in that position.)

So move to the right. Bring on the digits from the ones column. Only compare the two numbers that are competing for second place.

165

Compare them: A five is in the ones position in both the numbers 45.3 and 45. So again it's a tie.

Move to the right. Bring on the digits from the tenths column. Look at just the two numbers that are competing for second place.

Compare them: It's a three versus a zero, so finally you have a second-place winner.

You know that 45.0 was competing with 45.3. It lost that competition, but the other number, 0.301, wasn't even close, so you know that 45.0 comes in third. So the order of the four numbers is: 234.898, 45.3, 45.0, and finally 0.301. In a math sentence you would write 234.898 > 45.3 > 45.0 > 0.301.

Now you try a few problems.

1. Using the given table, order the teams from the most goals scored per game to the least. Do a Unit Check, Line 'Em Up, and Compare left to right.

Soccer Goals Per Game	
Team	**Average Score Per Game**
Blue Shark	4.0
Tigers	3.1
Hurricanes	3.12
Troubleshooters	3.9

2. Write in order from smallest to largest the following numbers:

   0.025 0.67 0.25 0.829

   a._____ b._____ c._____ d._____

3. Is the number 0.760 equal to, greater than, or less than 0.76?

4. Write in order from smallest to largest the following numbers:

   0.104 0.014 0.140

   a._____ b._____ c._____

4. a. 0.014, b. 0.104, c. 0.140
3. 0.760 is equal to 0.76.
2. a. 0.025, b. 0.25, c. 0.67, d.0.829
1. The order of the soccer teams is Blue Sharks, Troubleshooters, Hurricanes, and finally, Tigers.

Great job! Now let's check in with Shabang and see how she's doing.

"Ms. Shabang?" Egweena said, hurrying over to where Shabang stood waiting. "Are you okay, ma'am?"

"Yes, of course, dear," Shabang said, trying to act as if she actually knew where she was. "Let's go find the others. Do you remember the way?"

"Sure," Egweena said, bouncing off down the hall.

Shabang breathed a sign of relief. What would she have done if Egweena hadn't known the way? The fuzzy times were happening more and more frequently.

What was the last thing she remembered? Sitting on the bed? Looking at three keys? Shabang shuddered.

Three separated keys.

She started to fade—no, she wouldn't let it happen. She had to stay strong.

They turned a corner and stepped into a lobby area. Mr. Little was standing on his stool, watching. By habit Shabang counted, one, two, until she reached the magic number of twenty. Good. All the children were present, but why was Sticky's arm in a sling?

She had no idea, and that's what bothered her most.

Chapter 14
As Easy as Pie

"To keep things simple," the tour guide said to the class, "marbles are made from cooled glass that is rolled into balls of different sizes."

"Is that what the machine is doing?" Sticky asked, pointing to a huge furnace dropping molten glass through a chute onto a forming table.

"Exactly. Years ago everything was done by hand, with a kind of scissors that cut and pressed a rod of glass into a round cup."

Mr. Little smiled. The kids were engaged, and Ms. Shabang was acting more like her regular self.

"Mr. Little, did you hear that?" Sticky asked, pulling on Mr. Little's sleeve."

"No I didn't, Sticky," Mr. Little admitted. "Tell me."

"Used to be in the old days, kids who played marbles were juvenile delinquents, and I love marbles. So you think that's why I'm in trouble so much?"

"No, Sticky," Mr. Little said, trying to hide his smile. "You're a good kid."

Sticky took off, pushing his way to the front of the line. "MR. LITTLE! STICKY CUT!" several voices protested, and Mr. Little sighed.

He hoped Sticky could stay out of trouble for just a bit longer. All that was left was seeing how the marbles were packaged. Sometimes they were sorted by their sizes, like 0.635 cm, 1.25 cm, 2.5 cm, and 3.5 cm (cm stands for centimeters, which is a metric measurement), and sometimes they were sorted by color. But once the class saw that part of the process, they'd get on the bus and head back to school.

The sooner they get started on their tour, the sooner they'll get done. So while Mr. Little gets his students lined up, let's talk more about lining numbers up when we add and subtract decimals.

Just like you are an experienced decimal comparer, you also have added and subtracted decimals before.

Everyone likes to add decimals if it involves money and to subtract them if it involves subtracting someone else's money. And adding and subtracting decimals is almost exacting like adding and subtracting whole numbers except for one teensy, tiny, itsy, bitsy, little—

●

DARING DOT

When you add and subtract decimals, the only thing different is you have to keep track of the decimal's place. Unfortunately, this can be harder than it sounds.

170

So when an important addition or subtraction problem falls out of the sky, what do you do?

After you run for cover, the first thing you should do is a *Unit Inspection*. Remember, it also doesn't make sense to add 0.235 meters + 3.43 centimeters or 4.5 oz and 0.23 pounds. So always stop and inspect the units. If they aren't the same, convert them into like units.

Second up is *Line 'Em Up*.

When you line up the numbers on their decimals, you line up all the other place values as well.

Tens	Ones	Daring Dot	Tenths	Hundredths
	3	.	4	3
2	3	.	5	

The hundredths are in a line ready to be added.

The tenths are in a line ready to be added up.

All the digits are in a line with other digits with the same place value.

$$\begin{array}{r} 3.43 \\ + \ 23.5 \\ \hline \end{array}$$

Wait! You could have a problem. If you look at the numbers just mentioned, it would be easy for the five to just slide over. After all, there is nothing to stop it. If it slides, the sliding will continue until all the numbers are out of whack.

Talk about confusing! To keep things clear, it's a good idea to fill the empty places in a number with zeroes when you add and subtract decimals. The zero stops any unwelcome sliding.

After you Line 'Em Up, the third step is *Do It!*

There's nothing fancy about this step. Add 'em or subtract 'em just like you would a whole number, but when you write the digits, make sure you come straight down.

Next up is *Dot It*! Put the Daring Dot in its proper place. If you've done everything correctly up to this point, let gravity bring the Daring Dot straight down.

And finally, the last step is to *Check It* by estimating.

It is especially important when you are working with decimals to make sure the decimal point is in the right place. Just ask Elexus Estimator.

Thanks, Elexus. The number twenty-seven is close to 26.93, so we know we got the decimal point in the correct place.

Estimating is very important when you work with decimals. Often, to estimate decimal calculations, you round or truncate to the nearest whole number before you estimate.

One last thing about adding and subtracting decimals. When you do add and subtract them, you also borrow and carry like whole numbers. Sometimes this is called regrouping.

Okay, let's try these steps out with a money problem. Say you had $12.45, and then your grandmother gave you $25.25 for your birthday. How much money do you now have?

Subtracting with decimals works the same way as adding. Say you need to save $49.99 to buy the neatest and coolest game on the planet. So far you have $36.89. How much do you need to earn to have enough to buy the game? Assume it's a tax-free day, and no tax will be charged.

Since both amounts represent money, the units are the same. Line 'Em Up, Do It, and then Dot It:

$$\begin{array}{r} \$49.99 \\ -\ 36.89 \\ \hline \$13.10 \end{array}$$

Finally, Check It. Estimating the final answer by rounding each amount to the nearest dollar would give you $50 – $37 = $13, so $13.10 is a good answer.

See? It's easy! Even if someone asked, "Can you add five hundred fifty-six thousand four hundred fifty-six and three million two hundred thirty-four thousand three hundred forty-two ten-millionths plus four thousand three hundred forty-three and three million five hundred thirty-four thousand three hundred forty-five ten-millionths?" You'd say—Huh?

Yes, of course. After they repeated the number a few times, then you'd say...

Great job! Now try these problems:

1. What is three tenths + 3.4?
2. What if you have a whole pie and five tenths is taken away?
3. What is 6.78 – 5.6?
4. In the following table, fill in the missing decimal numbers that needed to be added or subtracted from the number to get the next number.

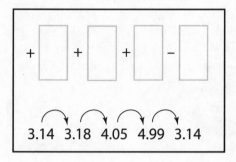

1. $0.3 + 3.4 = 3.7$;
2. $1.0 - 0.5 = 0.5$;
3. $6.78 - 5.6 = 1.18$;
4. $3.14 + 0.04 = 3.18, 3.18 + \overline{0.87} = 4.05,$
   $4.05 + 0.94 = 4.99, 4.99 - \overline{1.85} = 3.14$

177

Super!
Now let's go back to the marble factory.

"That's okay, Mr. Little. You can let go," Sticky said, pulling away.

"No, Sticky. You are walking with me until we get on the bus."

"I just want to see something," Sticky said.

Chapter 15
Turbo Dot Speed

Rat-a-tat-tat.

"Take cover," the tour guide yelled, ducking behind a nearby pillar.

Marbles shot out of the machine at an alarming speed.

Rat-a-tat-tat.

Rat-a-tat-tat.

"Sticky, what have you done?" Mr. Little scolded.

"I'm sorry. I didn't know." Sticky looked like he was about to cry, and Mr. Little let up. No use making things worse. He could talk to the boy later. For now he had to figure out a way to get the class back to the bus without anyone getting hurt.

A group of workers carrying a toolbox had gathered at the back of the machine.

"How many marbles will it make?" Mr. Little called.

One of the workers picked up a megaphone and held it to his lips. "The stop lever broke. We have to find a tool that can twist the bolt and turn it off."

Rat-a-tat-tat.

"How many marbles?" Mr. Little shouted again. Maybe the worker hadn't understood the question.

"If we can't find a tool, it'll run until it uses up all the glass," the head worker called back. "We just put in 300 pounds of glass and each marble uses about 0.1 ounces."

Rat-a-tat-tat.

It was so noisy Mr. Little could hardly hear himself breathe, and he certainly couldn't think. How many marbles would it make before it stopped? Would the marbles cover them before the machine stopped?

"Mr. Little, I'm scared, sir," Egweena said.

"It's okay," he told her with as much confidence as he could muster. "How about if we call in the superheroes?"

"They'll never hear us!" Sticky said, rubbing his bottom. It still smarted from the marble shot.

"Dixie will. She has super hearing," Egweena shot back with feminine pride, and Mr. Little smiled. At least the kids were thinking about something besides flying marbles.

"Let's all call together," Mr. Little said. He had no idea if Dixie would hear or not, but it was their only chance.

"On the count of three," Sticky said yelling over the noise.

Let's hope Dixie is where she will hear the call! Who knows how many marbles the machine will shoot out at turbo speed before it stops.

And speaking of turbo speed, when you learned how to multiply fractions, you learned multiplication can be thought of as either turbo addition or the great grouper. Keeping these ideas in the back of your mind will help while you learn how to multiply decimals. Overall it is easy, just three steps: Do It, Dot It, and Check It.

So when a multiplication problem comes your way…

You simply forget about the decimal and Do It.

To add turbo speed you need to use your multiplication tables. Fortunately, as with fractions, there are no new multiplication tables to learn, just the same old ones you hopefully know well.

So what does 5×0.6 look like from your fives multiplication table? Forget about the zones and decimals for a minute and Do It. Multiply 5×6. Then when you get your anwers, Dot It.

How? For the answer to this question and many more, we go to the expert herself, Dixie Dot.

TO FIND THE CORRECT PLACE, COUNT HOW MANY DECIMAL PLACES YOU TOOK OUT WHEN YOU MULTIPLIED.

The number of digits in the Part Zone in the question need to be in the Part Zone in the answer.

PART ZONE QUESTION = PART ZONE ANSWER

Count the decimal places in both numbers.

The number 5 has 0 decimal places and can also be thought of as $\frac{5}{1}$, while 0.6 has one decimal place and can also be thought of as $\frac{6}{10}$. (You will learn more about this in Chapter 16.)

So 0 decimal places + 1 decimal place = 1 decimal place.

Take your answer thirty. Roll the decimal point over one place to the left.

$$3\underset{\curvearrowright}{.}0.$$

Roll one place over

$$5 \times 0.6 = 3.0$$

You can understand why you rolled the decimal over if you look at the same problem written as a fraction: $5 \times 0.6 = \frac{5}{1} \times \frac{6}{10} = \frac{30}{10}$. You can reduce the answer to $\frac{3}{1} = 3.0$.

Now the last step: Check It

This is where you think about what multiplication really means. Think of the problem first as either 0.6 added to itself five times or 0.6 of a group of five. If you use the group approach, the decimal 0.6 is a little more than 0.5 which is equal to $\frac{1}{2}$. The answer would be a little more than

$\frac{1}{2}$ of a group of five, so it makes sense that the answer

would be 3.0. (To check your answer you can also divide 3.0 ÷ 5 or 3.0 ÷ 0.6.)

Now you've learned that $5 \times 0.6 = 3.0$.

Do you know that $5 \times 0.06 = 0.3$? You still multiply $5 \times 6 = 30$, but this time when you Dot It you roll over two places instead of one.

And $5 \times 0.006 = 0.03$.

And $5 \times 0.0006 = 0.003$.

See how it works?

To multiple a decimal, multiply the numbers like you would without the decimals, and then Dot It.

Got it? Try it!

$$0.9 \times 4$$
$$0.09 \times 4$$
$$0.009 \times 4$$

$0.9 \times 4 = 3.6;\ 0.09 \times 4 = 0.36;\ 0.009 \times 4 = 0.036$

Now you understand the basics of multiplying decimals, so if you run into a difficult problem—

Don't be scared.
Just Do It!

$$\begin{array}{r} 23.456 \\ \times\ \ \ 0.12 \\ \hline 46912 \\ 234560 \\ \hline 281472 \end{array}$$

Now Dot It! How many places over does the dot need to move?

$$2 \quad 8 \quad 1 \quad 4 \quad 7 \quad 2 \, .$$

$$5 \quad 4 \quad 3 \quad 2 \quad 1$$

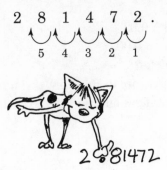

2.81472

There you go!

The answer is 2.81472. Check it by estimating. Remember, the problem was 23.456×0.12. One good estimation would be $20 \times \dfrac{1}{10} = \dfrac{20}{10} = 2$.

And now that you have that concept down, let's switch gears to division.

Division is the flip side of multiplication. Division in a nut shell is splitting an object, or group of objects, into equal parts or groups. You can also think of it as turbo subtraction.

So as you learn about decimal division, keep the turbo subtraction and division grouper in the back of your mind.

As you did with multiplication, let's start with numbers that are part of your multiplication and division tables. Here comes a problem now.

First up: Move Out the Divisor Decimal. The divisor is the number after the ÷ symbol, so in this case it is 0.8. The divisor is also the number of groups. Decimals in the divisor are tricky, but you can't pretend it's not there like you did when you multiplied. When you are dividing, you must move the decimal point out once and for all by making an equivalent equation without a decimal.

Remember how you did this? You multiplied or divided both the numerator and denominator by identical numbers and got an equivalent fraction. Well, since fractions are a form of division, you can get an equivalent equation by multiplying both numbers in the division equation by the same number.

$$40 \div 0.8 = 400 \div 8 = 4000 \div 80$$

Amazingly, they all have the same answer. To help you understand this better, think of it in terms of money. Forty dollars divided into groups of eight dimes will have the same answer as 400 dollars divided into groups of eight dollars.

Now let's try it on our problem $40 \div 0.8 =$ _____. Multiply each side by ten.

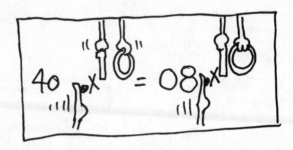

Another way to think of multiplying by ten is to simply move the decimal point over one position in each number. Don't believe? Watch.

$$40 \times 10 = 400$$
$$0.8 \times 10 = 8$$

And here are a few other numbers:

$$1.234 \times 10 = 12.34$$
$$0.945 \times 10 = 9.45$$

Instead of multiplying both numbers in a division equation by ten, you simply move the decimal point of both numbers one place to the right.

But what if there is more than one digit in the divisor that has wandered into the Part Zone?

3.45

How would you get rid of the decimal places in these problems?

$$12 \div 3.45$$
$$54 \div 0.987$$
$$3 \div 0.0345$$

If you can move the decimal points one place to the right, why can't you move them two places to the right as long as you do it for both numbers in the equation?

The answer is you can.

It's a decimal dance, and both decimal points have to step to the right the same amount; otherwise, they will step on each other's toes.

So $12 \div 3.45$ becomes $1,200 \div 345$.
$54 \div 0.987$ becomes $54,000 \div 987$.
$3 \div 0.0345$ becomes $30,000 \div 345$.

So you removed the decimal points and ended up with the equation $400 \div 8$. What's next? Divide as usual. Remember to put the decimal in the answer directly above the decimal point of the number you are dividing.

$$8\overline{)400.}$$

$$50.$$

Finally, the last step is to Check It! In the past, you've used Elexus Estimator to help you check your answer. You can use her for decimal division also, but the best way to check division is to multiply. If $400 \div 8 = 50$, then 50×8 should equal 400. Also, go back to the original equation and put in the answer. If $40 \div 0.8 = 50$, then 50×0.8 should be equal to 40.

Check it with the decimal multiplication you learned earlier in this chapter.

Remember, multiplication and division are inverse operations, so they go back and forth like this.

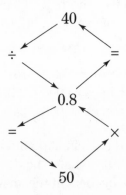

Okay, now you try a decimal division problem. How about $4.56 \div 3$?

Since the decimal is not in the divisor, you don't need to get rid of the decimal. Just make sure it is lined up when you go through your long division.

$$\begin{array}{r} 1.52 \\ 3\overline{)4.56} \\ \underline{3} \\ 15 \\ \underline{15} \\ 6 \\ \underline{6} \end{array}$$

Here are a couple more division problems:

1. $50 \div 0.5$
2. $1 \div 0.25$
3. And finally, how many marbles will the machine shoot out before it stops? The problem is 300 pounds ÷ 0.1 ounce.

1. $50 \div 0.5 = 500 \div 5 = 100$; **2.** $1 \div 0.25 = 100 \div 25 = 4$ (notice how this is the same as one dollar divided by 25 cents); **3.** If you convert the pounds to ounces, the problem becomes 4,800 ounces ÷ 0.1 ounce = 48,000.

Holy Moley, as Mr. Little would say, 48,000 is a lot of marbles. Hopefully Dixie will hear their call for help.

Dixie Dot couldn't believe her eyes! Right in front of her were southern peas, squash, yams, peppers, parsnips, beets—everything she'd been craving.

She glanced over at Silver, happily enjoying some of the best barbecue in town. He'd probably go back for seconds when he was done, which gave her plenty of time to shop.

She picked up a large onion and sniffed. It had a delightful, delicate aroma, a Vidalia onion, for sure. She resisted the urge to bite it like an apple. It was probably sweet enough, but she'd better pay first. In fact, she could get several, make relish and dressing and salsa—

Dixie tilted her head to the right and froze. Voices crying for help, but what else? Gunfire?

RAT - A - TAT - TAT
RAT - A - TAT - TAT

She looked up and saw Silver, standing with Mongrel, both staring at her, waiting.

"Trouble," she said, taking Silver's hand and letting him pull her up.

"Marble Factory?" Silver asked, pulling out his keys.

That was it, the rat-a-tat-tat sound. Dixie nodded. Something was terribly wrong.

She dropped the onion onto the pile and ran toward the car. The Mathopolis Farmer's Market would have to wait.

Chapter 16
Converts

Wow! The superheroes really have their work cut out for them this time, but surely there is more than one way to stop the marble machine. And just like there is more than one way to stop a machine, there is more than one way to change fractions to decimals and decimals to fractions.

The word for changing decimals to fractions or fractions to decimals is *conversion*. So what does the word *conversion* or the phrase *to convert* mean?

Convert means to change something into a different form. That's what fractions and decimals are, two different forms or ways of saying the same thing.

The more you work with fractions and decimals, the easier converting will get. Some conversions will feel comfortable, like your favorite pair of jeans. Often if the fractions or decimals are popular, or if an exact change isn't needed, benchmark fractions can be used to convert. Do you remember the popular benchmark fractions and decimals from earlier in the book?

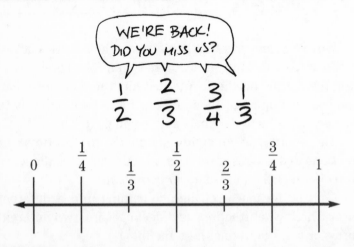

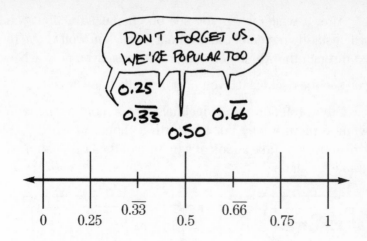

Well, these popular fractions and popular decimals are simply different names for the same spots on the number line. It's like a girl having the name of Patricia and also being called Pat.

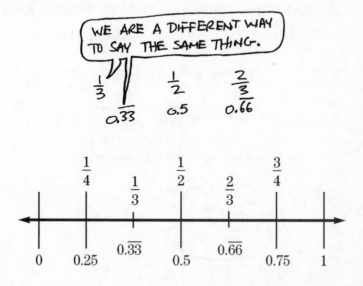

After a while, when you see one popular fraction, you will instantly remember its decimal name. You won't have to go through the whole conversion process. Even now, when you see the decimal 0.5 you may instantly know it is $\frac{1}{2}$.

Other fractions and decimals need more work, and while a picture may not be worth a thousand words, it's worth twenty. Take a look at a picture of the largest stick of gum ever made.

This stick of gum has been divided into 10 pieces. Each piece is $\frac{1}{10}$ of the total. Each piece is also 0.1 of the total. The fraction $\frac{1}{10}$ is the same as 0.1. They are the same amount.

Yes, 0.1 is said one tenth, just like $\frac{1}{10}$. This is because they are the same amount. And $\frac{2}{10}$ and 0.2 are also the same amount.

But what if Sticky took three of the pieces of gum? How would you write both the fraction and decimal amounts?

$\frac{3}{10}$ and 0.3

You can see how a fraction with the denominator of ten relates to a decimal. But what if you have to divide the stick of gum so a hundred kids can have a chew?

Each piece would be $\frac{1}{100}$. Each piece would be 0.01. The numbers are both said one hundredth. Now you can

197

see how a fraction with a denominator of 100 relates to a decimal, but more importantly, nobody gets as much gum.

If you understand this relationship between fractions and decimals, converting is easier. Let's start by looking at converting decimals to fractions. What does it take to make a fraction? Remember the bunk bed?

Yes, you need a numerator and a denominator to make a fraction. So how do you take the decimal number and pull out a numerator and a denominator?

The numerator is the decimal value without the Daring Dot. The denominator is the place value of the rightmost decimal number.

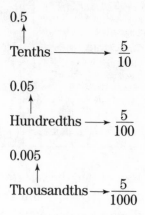

0.5
↑
Tenths ————→ $\dfrac{5}{10}$

0.05
↑
Hundredths ——→ $\dfrac{5}{100}$

0.005
↑
Thousandths —→ $\dfrac{5}{1000}$

Here's a harder problem: 0.56.

Ask yourself, what is the rightmost position of the decimal number? Pull its place value out. Its place value is the hundredths place, so make 100 your denominator.

Now put the 56 numerator over the 100 denominator. What do you get?

Yes! You get $\dfrac{56}{100} = \dfrac{28}{50} = \dfrac{14}{25}$ when it's reduced using the GCF of 4.

As always, when you get your answer, you Check It. Since your decimal is a two-digit decimal, your knowledge of money can help. The decimal 0.56 is like fifty-six cents, which is a little more than $\dfrac{1}{2}$ of a dollar. The fraction $\dfrac{14}{25}$ is also a little more than $\dfrac{1}{2}$ of a whole, because fourteen is a little more than half of twenty-five. So it looks like a good answer.

If you don't remember the place value names and can't look them up, here's a shortcut:

Now you try. Use either the *shortcut* or *pull-out-the-place-value* approach. In the table below, match the fractions on the left with the decimals on the right.

$1\frac{6}{10}$	0.3
$\frac{8}{100}$	0.25
$\frac{1}{10}$	1.6
$2\frac{7}{10}$	0.1
$\frac{25}{100}$	0.08
$\frac{3}{10}$	2.7

Answer Table

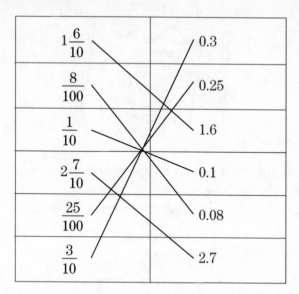

$1\dfrac{6}{10}$	0.3
$\dfrac{8}{100}$	0.25
$\dfrac{1}{10}$	1.6
$2\dfrac{7}{10}$	0.1
$\dfrac{25}{100}$	0.08
$\dfrac{3}{10}$	2.7

The final step of converting decimals to fractions is to reduce the fractions using the GCF, or Greatest Common Factor agent. Which of the above fractions need to be reduced?

The fractions $1\dfrac{6}{10}$, $\dfrac{8}{100}$, and $\dfrac{25}{100}$ all need to be reduced.

For example: $1\dfrac{6}{10}$ can be reduced to $1\dfrac{3}{5}$ if you divide the numerator and the denominator by the GCF of 2.

Now your turn. Convert $\dfrac{8}{10}$ and $\dfrac{25}{100}$.

$\dfrac{8}{10} = \dfrac{4}{5}$ when you divide the numerator and the denominator both by the GCF of 2. The fraction $\dfrac{25}{100} = \dfrac{1}{4}$ when you divide the numerator and the denominator both by the GCF of 25.

So here's a quick review of changing decimals to fractions:

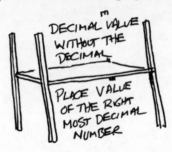

If, on the other hand, you want to change a fraction to a decimal, the process is totally different.

Some fractions are easy to convert to decimals.

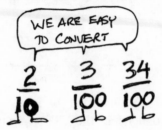

But, how do you know it's an easy fraction to convert? Because the fraction itself says it's easy when it has a denominator that is a power of ten. A power of ten denominator is a one followed only by zeroes.

So which of the following fractions have a power of ten denominator: $\frac{3}{10}$, $\frac{4}{100}$, $\frac{1}{101}$, $\frac{3}{15}$, $\frac{345}{1000}$ **and** $\frac{2}{21}$?

The following fractions have a denominator that is a power of ten: $\frac{3}{10}$, $\frac{4}{100}$, $\frac{345}{1000}$.

So when you have a power of ten denominator, what do you do? The power of ten denominator tells you the place value of the last decimal place. That's as far as the number can go to the right, no further.

If the denominator is not a power of ten, then quickly see if it can be changed into a power of ten. The fraction $\frac{2}{5}$ can easily become $\frac{4}{10}$ by multiplying both the numerator and denominator by two. Then it easily slips into decimal land as 0.4.

For fractions that don't have a power of ten denominator, it helps to keep in mind what you learned way back at the beginning of the book.

203

If you want to change fractions to decimals, you do the division. The fraction $\frac{1}{2}$ can be thought of as one-half or as 1 divided by 2.

$$\frac{1}{\div\ 2}$$

Just divide it!

$$2\overline{)1.0}$$

Of course it doesn't go without adding a zero to the one and making it ten. Then you know that $2 \times 5 = 10$.

$$\begin{array}{r} 0.5 \\ 2\overline{)1.0} \\ \underline{1.0} \\ 0 \end{array}$$

So $1 \div 2 = 0.5$.

That wasn't so bad, was it? You've converted $\frac{1}{2}$ into a decimal, but now that you have your answer, what do you do?

CHECK IT

Yes, reverse the problem and check the answer. If $1 \div 2 = 0.5$ then 0.5×2 should $= 1$. (Use your decimal multiplication skills to check, and you will see it's correct.)

When you are converting a fraction to a decimal, if you keep having a repeating remainder, stop. For example, $\frac{1}{3}$:

$$
\begin{array}{r}
0.33 \\
3{\overline{\smash{\big)}\,1.0}} \\
.9 \\
\overline{.10} \\
.09 \\
\overline{.01}
\end{array}
$$

Since the remainder is always one, you could divide forever and ever, like the marbles flying out of the machine. Instead of a never-ending dividing job, put a line above the threes to note that it is a repeating decimal.

Okay, now you know how to convert. Here are a few questions to make sure you understand what you're doing.

1. Sally bought $\frac{2}{3}$ of a pound of cheese and Judy bought 0.33 of a pound. Who bought more cheese, Sally or Judy?

2. Given the diagram below, what part of the whole is not shaded? Give the answer as both a decimal and a fraction.

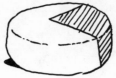

3. Given the fraction $\frac{1}{5}$, convert it to a decimal.

4. Convert the fraction $\frac{1}{4}$ into a decimal.

---

1. To solve this problem convert one or the other or use benchmark fractions. If you use benchmark fractions to convert, you know that $\frac{2}{3}$ of a pound of cheese is equal to $0.6\overline{6}$. $\frac{2}{3} > 0.33$, so Sally bought more.

2. $\frac{3}{4}$ of the area is not shaded and $\frac{3}{4} = \frac{73}{100} = 0.75$. You can either divide $3 \div 4$ to get this answer or use the benchmark fractions.

3. Convert $\frac{1}{5}$ by doing $1 \div 5 = 0.2$.

4. The fraction $\frac{1}{4}$ is $1 \div 4 = 0.25$ (notice the quarter connection).

Now, what about Dixie? Do you think she has been able to convert the marble machine from on to off?

"Now!" Silver said.

Dixie wrapped her fingers around the bolt and twisted.

Nothing. She tightened even more, straining, putting all her strength into the task. Finally the bolt yielded, slightly at first, and then more and more until she could move it forward in its slot as the lever had done, pushing it toward the off position.

Rat-a-tat-tat—rat-a-tat-ta—rat-a—

It was over.

Silver blocked one last marble and dropped his arms to his side.

"Good job," he said, smiling at Dixie. She was bent over at the waist, breathing as if she'd run a marathon.

"Woof," Mongrel agreed from the door, and he walked over and rubbed his head against Dixie's hand.

"Children, Dixie and Silver stopped the machine," Mr. Little called, standing up to peer over the barricade. "Let's get on the bus."

Slowly the students emerged from among the piles and started to assess their wounds.

"Boy, that was fun!" Sticky said, practically bouncing out of the marbles. "Do you think they'd mind if I took a few of these?"

"Now, Sticky. They aren't yours," said Mr. Little.

"But they are on the floor!" said Sticky.

"I don't want to go on any more field trips, sir," Egweena said quietly. "It's too scary."

"You're okay," Mr. Little said, patting her on the back. "How about if we stop at the ice cream store on the way back?"

"I just want to go home," she said, and Mr. Little nodded. He definitely understood that feeling.

"Okay," he said. "Just follow Ms. Shabang—." Mr. Little looked around. Where was she, anyway? "Ms. Shabang?" he called. "Ms. Shabang?"

"Marbles—Marbles—"

Everyone looked around.

"It's okay, Ms. Shabang," Dixie said. "We'll have you out in no time. Are you hurt?"

"Marbles," Shabang called.

"I know," Dixie answered. "Marbles are everywhere. That was quite a scare."

Chapter 17

All's Well That Ends Well

"Sorry fellas," Dixie said, waving to the workers as she put down her bin. "Have to go solve a crime." She jogged over to where Silver was standing.

He seemed like he was about to spill the beans. As soon as she was close enough to hear, he started whispering.

"You're kidding me," Dixie said as she came up to his side. Silver shook his head, and both looked over at Newsie/Shabang.

"Let's check it out," Dixie said, and the two strolled toward Newsie.

Newsie's face wrinkled in annoyance when she saw them.

"Hi, there," Dixie called when they made eye contact. "Decided not to take the bus back to school?"

"Don't try being nice to me. I'm not going to fall for an ol' brownie trick," Newsie said, pulling way.

"Ms. Shabang?" Silver said, softly. "Are you there?"

"NO," Newsie cried, but with the grace of one sure of her convictions, Shabang straightened her back and assumed the ballet position five.

"I'm here," Shabang said, doing three plies. "I understand now."

"Understand what?" Dixie asked, slipping her arm around Shabang's shoulder.

"That it's time to do the right thing. I didn't want the mayor to get hurt, but she, that Newsie girl, wouldn't let me give the keys back."

"I know." Dixie spoke softly, calmly. "You're like a fraction, two halves of one person. And we can get help to make you one person again. Okay?"

"She buried them, you know," Shabang went on, "so I couldn't get to them. Only now I know. When the marbles flew around, over and over again, marbles and marbles—I can't explain—I just knew."

"What?" Silver asked, still keeping his voice soft.

"About Newsie, and where she buried the keys."

"The mayor's in real danger," Dixie said, massaging Shabang's neck. "Will you help us out?"

Shabang nodded. "I just didn't want the three divided, you know, split apart."

"I understand," Dixie said. "We will take all of them, all three, to the bank."

Shabang stiffened again, as if in a mighty struggle, then relaxed.

"Newsie isn't happy," she said, her voice now hoarse. "But I must tell you something so I can rest." And with that she leaned in and whispered all she knew.

"You did the right thing," Dixie said. She looked Shabang straight in the eye. "And you *are* going to be okay."

"Thank you," Shabang said, giving Dixie a weak smile. "I'll just wait here until you get back."

"No, thank *you*," Dixie replied. "You have helped us so much." She gave Shabang a quick hug, and then turned and ran after Silver who was already at the car.

"Silver, how did you know?" Dixie asked as they sped toward the nursery.

"Fingerprint," Silver said. "Shabang's."

"The one off the worksheet at the bank?"

Silver nodded. "Took to MPD."

"So that's who you were talking to on your cell? The police?" Dixie asked.

Silver nodded again. "Fractions mess with her mind. She can't control it."

"We'll get her help. She'll be okay," Dixie said. "Now, though, we need to save Mayor Marbles."

The foreman's fingers twitched as he wrapped his hand around the plunger. "Okay. This is it."

He took a deep breath, held it, flexed his shoulders and—

"Stop," Silver yelled out the window of the car as it rounded the corner. "KEYS!"

"Okay! Let's get the mayor out," the bank manager said, coming forward with Trusty Dusty at his side. Both had huge smiles, as if Christmas had come early.

"Where did you find them?" Trusty asked. Everyone leaned in eagerly for the answer.

"Well," Dixie said, thinking quickly. She didn't want to speak badly of Shabang who would be just fine soon. "They were buried at the nursery."

"Under vines," Silver added, as they arrived at the vault, and everyone focused on the keys.

One by one he inserted them into the appropriate lock, turning the last one until the keypad lit up.

Without hesitation the bank manager typed in the appropriate code and the motor hummed.

"Mayor Marbles? Sir? Are you okay?" Dixie asked, stepping into the vault.

And once again our superheroes have saved the day for the citizens of Mathopolis. It is time to celebrate!

FROM THE KITCHEN OF DIXIE'S MOM:
SOUTHERN BROWNIES

2 SQ UNSWEETENED CHOCOLATE (2 OZ.)

⅓ C. BUTTER

1 C. GRANULATED SUGAR

2 EGGS

¾ C. FLOUR

½ TSP. BAKING POWDER

½ TSP. SALT

½ C. CHOPPED WALNUTS

MELT BUTTER AND CHOCOLATE OVER A
LOW HEAT. BEAT IN EGGS AND SUGAR. ADD FLOUR,
BAKING POWDER AND SALT. STIR IN NUTS.
BAKE IN A GREASED 8×8×2 PAN AT
350 DEGREES FOR 30 TO 35 MINUTES. ENJOY!

Wow! Can you believe it?

Not long ago Silver and Dixie invited you to join them in the Fraction and Decimal World. You've met bank robbers, secret agents, and circus performers. You traveled with Mr. Little and his gang on their ill-fated field trips, and learned about Whole Zones and Part Zones along the way. You've seen Dixie Dot and Silver Splitter save the day many times. Just think of all you've accomplished, and give yourself a pat on the back.

You've earned it!

Barron's presents...

Adventures In
MATHOPOLIS

Estimating and Measuring _____

Karen Ferrell, Catherine Weiskopf, and Linda Powley, Illustrated by Tom Kerr
Elementary-level math becomes an exercise in fun when kids open this
cartoon-illustrated fantasy. The story's cast of characters includes Lostis
Marbles, the mayor of Mathopolis, who loves numbers but usually gets
them all mixed up . . . his assistant Trusty Dusty, who helps the mayor keep track of his math
mix-ups . . . Mongrel Smith, the town's stray dog . . . and two math superheroes, who use different
methods to solve problems. The Superheroes are Elexus Estimator, who is quick at estimating volume,
height, weight, and the like . . . and Maverick Measurer, who values accuracy above all else when
making math calculations. A mysterious character shows up in town, and the problems he brings with
him can be solved by applying math principles. The math Superheroes show young readers how.
Students will enjoy the funny episodes as they encounter one math word
problem after another. Meanwhile, they effortlessly learn to think,
calculate, and come up with the right answers. (Ages 9–12)

Paperback, 224 pp., ISBN-13: 978-0-7641-3867-6

The Great Polygon Caper _____

Karen Ferrell
Mayor Lostis Marbles is back again and looking for more help in solving
his problems. But now the superhero and problem solver is the fifteen-
year-old, skateboard-riding Kent Clark, also known as Edge Master. The
villains are the Shiftless gang, led by Shiftless Shereé, a mysterious
woman with long, red fingernails, and her brother Ambrose Addemup. In a series of funny, fictional
episodes, Edge Master helps the hapless mayor solve problems involving angles, polygons, triangles,
quadrilaterals, squares, prisms, and pyramids. He also demonstrates how to calculate the volume of
solid objects. Kids will be entertained as they familiarize themselves with the fundamentals of
geometry. (Ages 9–12)

Paperback, approx. 208 pp., ISBN-13: 978-0-7641-4041-9

Please visit **www.barronseduc.com**
to view current prices and to order books

Barron's Educational Series, Inc.
250 Wireless Blvd.
Hauppauge, NY 11788
Order toll-free: 1-800-645-3476
Order by fax: 1-631-434-3217

In Canada:
Georgetown Book Warehouse
34 Armstrong Ave.
Georgetown, Ont. L7G 4R9
Canadian orders: 1-800-247-7160
Fax in Canada: 1-800-887-1594

(#161) R 1/09

Honest, Kids! It's fun to learn . . .

BARRON'S PAINLESS JUNIOR SERIES

Teachers in grades 3 and 4 will appreciate these new classroom helpers. Designed to resemble titles in Barron's **Painless Series**—which are used in middle school and high school classrooms—Painless Junior books feature larger page sizes, amusing illustrations, games, puzzles, and an approach to their subjects that reflects third- and fourth-grade curricula. The purpose of these books is to inject an element of enjoyment into subjects that many younger students find either boring or mystifying. Kids' understanding will improve as they have fun learning.

Each book: Paperback, approximately 208 pp.,
7 13/16" × 10"

PAINLESS JUNIOR: GRAMMAR

Marciann McClarnon, M.S., Illustrated by Tracy Hohn
Teachers and students will value this instructive and entertaining journey to *Grammar World*, where kids have fun while they develop their facility in correct English usage. Boys and girls learn about different kinds of sentences; nouns, pronouns, adjectives, and several other parts of speech; verbs, prepositions, prepositional phrases, conjunctions, and interjections; punctuation, capitalization, and abbreviations.
ISBN 978-0-7641-3561-3

PAINLESS JUNIOR: WRITING

Donna Christina Oliverio, M.S.
Kids travel with Sammy Octopus on a reading and writing adventure. They are encouraged to try different methods of writing and see which way works best for them. They also learn the value of revising and editing, engage in activities that help them make good word choices, and get practice in descriptive writing, letter writing, report writing, poetry, and much more.
ISBN 978-0-7641-3438-8

PAINLESS JUNIOR: MATH

Margery Masters
Young students learn to comprehend the many uses of numbers as they engage in number games and fun-to-solve puzzles. Starting with counting, they advance to arithmetic, fractions, decimals, and the different ways of measuring.
ISBN-13: 978-0-7641-3450-0

PAINLESS JUNIOR: SCIENCE

Wendie Hensley, M.A., and Annette Licata, M.A.
Find out how plants and animals are closely connected with each other as parts of the Earth's ecosystem. Discover the magic of light, and see how it is reflected and refracted. There's just as much magic in magnetism and electricity, and this book explains how they work and how they're related.
ISBN 978-0-7641-3719-8

PAINLESS JUNIOR: ENGLISH FOR SPEAKERS OF OTHER LANGUAGES

Jeffrey Strausser and José Paniza
This textbook for both children and adults who speak English as their second language acquaints students with correct English sentence construction, parts of speech, capitalization, punctuation, and spelling, and offers extra tips on how to expand one's English language vocabulary.
ISBN 978-0-7641-3984-0